Eyes Right

EYES RIGHT

Confessions from a Woman Marine

TRACY CROW

University of Nebraska Press: Lincoln and London

Acknowledgments for previously published
material appear on page ix, which
constitutes an extension of the copyright page.

All photographs are courtesy of the author,
unless otherwise indicated.

Library of Congress Cataloging-in-Publication Data

Crow, Tracy.
Eyes right: confessions from a woman Marine /
Tracy Crow.   p. cm.
ISBN 978-0-8032-3504-5 (cloth: alk. paper)
1. Crow, Tracy. 2. Women marines—United
States—Biography. 3. United States. Marine Corps—
Women—Biography. 4. United States. Marine
Corps—Officers—Biography. I. Title.
VE25.C77A3 2012   359.9'6092—dc23   [B]
2011033393

Set in Scala by Bob Reitz.
Designed by Ashley Muehlbauer.

For my daughter, Morgan,
and women warriors everywhere

Acknowledgments

If not for one woman, this book would never have taken shape.

Several years ago, I was enrolled in an undergraduate memoir-writing workshop with Dr. Helen Wallace at Eckerd College. On the stroll to our cars one evening after class, Helen asked about my military experience. I shared a few stories. In the middle of the parking lot, Helen stopped me and asked why I wasn't writing down these stories for her class. I said I didn't think anyone would care.

Since no one can say no to Helen Wallace, I set about to write the first essay, which was the experience of fighting my way onto the rifle range to qualify as the beat reporter for John Hopkins's Fifth Marines and about going to the desert with Hopkins. Helen has since become a dear friend and colleague, and she and her husband, Peter, have seen me through tough times. I'm so grateful for their love and encouragement.

I would also like to thank Cindy Liss for her years of encouragement. Cindy was the first reader to explain what I was actually writing. "Really?" I said one day on the phone after she'd detailed the themes. "All that's in there?" Sometimes writers are too wrapped up in the words and how those words form sentences and how those sentences work structurally to see the forest of their themes. If only every writer had a Cindy Liss.

And a Jeff Hess. Jeff's support and keen editing skills have proven invaluable through the years. Thanks, Jeff, for all the long hours on uncomfortable chairs at Starbucks.

I am especially grateful to my editor at the University of Nebraska Press, Heather Lundine, for her guidance and overwhelming support. Thanks also to Bridget Barry, Sara Springsteen, Cara Pesek, and the entire University of Nebraska Press team, along with freelance editor Sue Breckenridge.

I met C.J. Walters, a former Marine, at Camp Pendleton in the early eighties, and she is the quintessential woman warrior. Thanks, C.J., for your enduring friendship and tireless devotion and faith in all my endeavors. I'm also indebted to Libby Oberg, another woman warrior who, for some reason, believes in me more than I believe in myself. Thanks to former Marines: Walter E. Boomer, Monique Fleming, Joaquin Gracida, Phil Hartranft, Carl E. Mundy, Henry C. Stackpole III, and Russ and Debbie Thurman.

Carol Fant, Jessica Handler, Margaret MacInnis, Dee Perez, Sarah Campbell, and Sally Drumm deserve thanks for their workshop help with this project during graduate school at Queens University of Charlotte and for their constant support since. I'm also grateful to Fred Leebron, codirector of the Queens MFA program, for his unending encouragement and for keeping his promise about developing "a warm community of writers" at Queens University, a community that cheers the tiniest writing success and uplifts above the mountain of rejections associated with the business of writing. Thanks to Kathryn Rhett, J. D. Dolan, Suzannah Lessard, Rebecca McClanahan, Pinckney Benedict, Michael Kobre, Peter Stitt, Abigail Thomas, Robert Polito, and Cathy Smith Bowers for their faculty encouragement and support of this project throughout graduate school, and beyond.

For encouraging me to examine certain, even painful, motives within this story, thank you, Michael Steinberg. Gratitude also goes to Jeremy Katz for his early belief in this project and everything I've written since.

Heartfelt appreciation to Janet Adkins, Sterling Watson, and the entire Eckerd College community and to my devoted former students and colleagues at the University of Tampa.

I want to thank Morgan's father for loving me the best way he knew how and for his role in producing such a special daughter. I'm also grateful to the entire Crow family for reasons too numerous and too personal to list here.

Thanks to Brian and my entire family. To Morgan, my mother, and my brother, especially—thank you for trusting me with your stories, for this book is as much yours as mine.

And a special thanks to my husband, Mark, who brings immeasurable joy and laughter to my life every day.

The events within this book are true. How I wish many of them weren't. Certain names, however, have been changed or omitted to protect privacy, or because, regrettably, I couldn't recall them.

An earlier version of part 1, chapter 8 was published as "Kyoko's Mirror," *Literary Mama* (April 2007), http://www.literarymama .com/creativenonfiction/archives/2007/04/kyokos-mirror .html.

A portion of part 2, chapter 5 was previously published as "Natural Selection," in *Home of the Brave*, ed. Jeffery Hess (Winston-Salem NC: Press 53, 2009), 175–90.

An earlier version of part 2, chapter 8 was published as "Shooting Azimuths," *Puerto del Sol* 40 (Summer 2005): 128–37.

Author's Note

Every Marine has a story. Every Marine a reason for enlisting, perhaps an even better one for leaving. This is my story. A combination of one part breaking ground with three parts breaking all the rules, for which there were painful consequences.

Eyes Right

ONE

★

When I was twenty-eight, younger than my daughter is today, I was facing the likelihood of a court-martial. I followed a Marine sergeant down a polished corridor, past the clacking of typewriters and murmurs behind the closed doors of Military Police Headquarters, and pretended to be unafraid, as if I had nothing to hide, as if on the way there that morning I hadn't seriously mapped out a plan for desertion. Inhaling and exhaling in the same forced rhythm of a runner pacing through a psychological wall, I was committed to a marathon of sorts, and so I was breathing in and breathing out, matching foot speed and cadence with the young Marine ahead of me: a machinated force, we were, matching left foot and right, left arm and right, until he pulled up short in front of a closed door. My toe stubbed against the heel of his boot. Acting politely unaware, he pushed open the door and stepped aside for me to enter. He wore well his role of consummate Marine, refusing the eye contact I was desperate to interpret.

"The captain will be with you shortly, Ma'am," he said.

I forced a smile. "Thank you, Sergeant." After he disappeared behind the closed door, I heard those machine-like limbs working their way back down the corridor.

This was March 1987. The year Prozac made its debut. Gasoline was eighty-nine cents a gallon; the cost to mail a letter, just twenty-four cents. Televangelist Jim Bakker had self-destructed, much the same way I had, by way of sex scandal.

The interrogation room at Military Police Headquarters was

battleship gray and the size of a child's bedroom. Under the single window, someone with a utilitarian mindset had shoved a gray metal desk; under the desk were two gray metal chairs so that interrogator and suspect were compelled to sit on the same side of the desk facing each other, or face out the window together. Which position, I wondered, would my interrogator choose?

The walls were devoid of the usual framed photographs that displayed various weaponry and aircraft, were even missing the typical reenlistment posters with their *Stay Marine!* messages. After ten years in the Marines, I seldom noticed the posters anymore, their propaganda blending into the environment like the green-and-tan camouflage uniforms we wore on field combat exercises. But, in this tiny interrogation room, the absence of reenlistment posters, the missing option of *Stay Marine!* felt conspicuous.

My heart was still running that marathon. My mind, however, was signaling that I should find some way to feign calmness, and so I leaned over the metal desk, finding the cold surface alarming against my feverish skin. I peered out the window on the pretense I was actually interested in the outdoor activity of the handful of Marines who were bundled in green field jackets against the mid-March frost. They were slowly walking the perimeter of the parking lot, policing for litter and cigarette butts. Before becoming an officer, I was enlisted and assigned to litter details. I wondered if the Marines below felt as I had—like a prisoner on work release.

Except for a few tall evergreens, the world surrounding Military Police Headquarters appeared as dismal and gray as the inside of the interrogation room. In the center of the parking lot stood the flagpole, and the flag, painfully conspicuous against the colorless sky, was whipping about at the mercy of the March cold front that had apparently gathered strength since my arrival, causing the flag's cables to clang now and then against the pole. This was the sort of morning that if at home, as I had been for two weeks already on house arrest, I might have been in the kitchen chopping carrots, celery, and onions for a cozy beef stew dinner that night with my husband and daughter. As it was, I had no plans for dinner that night. No plans for the rest of the day since abandoning my desertion fantasy of a new life in Canada. No plans for the day after this one; none for the rest of my life.

I was still leaning over the metal desk, watching Marines pick up litter, when the door of the interrogation room finally opened. A woman captain, wearing trousers and shiny oxfords the size of my husband's, entered. I straightened to attention, feeling ridiculously feminine and outmatched in my uniform choice of a skirt and high heels.

I knew this captain. Well, not knew her in the sense that we had shared anything other than salutes when passing each other in various parking lots around the air station. But I knew the woman who towered toward the dim fluorescent light on the ceiling in that interrogation room, the woman with slicked-back, white-blond hair, face Aryan cool and sharp, as the officer in charge of Military Police. "At ease, Warrant Officer," she said in a tone offering nothing for interpretation, her eye contact brief and hesitant. I placed my hands against the small of my back and waited while she juggled from one hand to the other a legal-sized yellow pad, a pen, and a tape recorder, placing each on the metal desk, and each object, the way everything has of occupying space, further reducing the already too small room.

After closing the door, she motioned for me to take a chair. I pulled from under the desk the closer of the two chairs. I don't know why; either the decision seemed obvious or I was too intimidated to break her sphere of personal space. The padding of the seat I had chosen was ripped. I sat, and when I raised my right leg to cross it over my left knee, the upturned tear of fabric jabbed into a muscle and tugged at my stocking so that I had no choice but to lower my foot back to the floor.

The captain pulled out the second chair. The seat was not ripped. "Good morning, Warrant Officer," she said, sitting.

"Good morning, Ma'am."

She popped open the compartment of the cassette recorder. Apparently satisfied to find a tape, she closed the compartment, and then, sliding the machine across the desk, she seemingly divided the room into her half and my half. "So, how are you holding up, Tracy?"

The sound of my first name reverberated throughout the room. I could count on both hands the number of times in ten years a military officer had spoken my first name. Each time had been a deliberate attempt at intimacy. Something like hope was beginning to course through my veins. "I'm okay, Ma'am . . . given the circumstances."

She had been scribbling across the top of the legal pad the way you do when your pen seems out of ink, but suddenly stopped to look up. She smiled with the ease of an ally. Then, reaching across her half of the desk to turn on the tape recorder, she said, in a voice louder than I thought necessary, "You have the right to remain silent. Anything you say can and will be used against you. Do you understand?"

I nodded, forgetting the tape recorder. She pointed to the machine.

I leaned closer. "Yes, Ma'am."

And just like that, while outside, Marines collected litter from around the parking lot of Military Police Headquarters, while two blocks away at my own office my Public Affairs staff—my former staff—debated, even argued, over the front-page photograph for the upcoming newspaper, while my husband, Tom, halfheartedly inspected ammunition bunkers as a distraction until my phone call, while our six-year-old daughter, Morgan, warmly tucked inside an overly bright and cheerful first-grade classroom, practiced simple addition or finger painted, the interrogation procedure regarding charges against me for conduct unbecoming an officer, which included adultery, was finally underway.

★

I was born with the sort of dark hair that turns the burnt-reddish shade you see on old junkyard dogs during the summer. I was born with the green eyes of my Scottish ancestry and the olive complexion of my Native American roots. What I wasn't born was a leader.

I wasn't born a college professor, a wife, a mother, or a Marine for that matter, anymore than my father was born an alcoholic—although everyone who knew him claimed he was a born salesman.

One summer night when I was about eleven, the escalation of voices from our living room coaxed me from the book I was reading in my bedroom. I slid in socks across my mother's waxed hardwood hallway toward the conversation in time to hear my father tell the door-to-door encyclopedia salesman that the problem with the pitch was that the salesman didn't know when to stop talking. "A good salesman," my father was lecturing, "knows when to shut up and hand the customer a pen." The exaggerated enthusiasm on the salesman's face quickly faded as if my father had taken one of my big, fat erasers to it. The salesman opened his briefcase and gathered his colored brochures from our coffee table, unaware that in three weeks my father would call him to order the encyclopedias as a Christmas present for my younger brother and me. "The only thing a salesman's got is his product," Dad was saying as the salesman hurried for the door. "You have to believe in what you're selling."

Believe in what you're selling. Fake it until you make it. These were the mantras I carried with me throughout my twenties, throughout that decade I was a Marine. So maybe my father *had* been born a salesman. What I know for certain is that father and daughter seemed born with a relentless drive to prove something—to themselves, maybe to the world. My father eventually drank away his drive, and his dreams soon dematerialized.

But in those early years in Roanoke, Virginia, in the picturesque valley surrounded by the Appalachian Mountains, my father was the No. 1 salesman in the Southeast. He sold milk store to store for PET in all its forms: evaporated, canned, and powdered. He drove a company car that my brother and I helped to choose each year from brochures our father brought home and passed around the dinner table for debate. One year, we chose a black Ford Galaxy with red pinstriping and tan cloth interior; another year it was the buttercup-yellow Chevrolet Caprice with white leather seats. The latter was chosen for our mother because we knew buttercup yellow was her favorite color.

On those nights when Dad's new car sat in the driveway, my brother and I would rush our parents through dinner and the clearing off the table for the family tradition that awaited us: the breaking in of the new car with its heady new car smell that my brother and I knew wouldn't last long against our parents' chain smoking. After my mother and I had washed and dried the last of the dishes, our family would pile into the new car for what always felt like a victory lap around Roanoke, looping around Mill Mountain for a glance at the giant neon star that flashed red in those days to signal a traffic death, white if all were safe.

Had we still been living in Roanoke when my father died two months before Tom and I married in 1979, the star would have flashed red for him. But by then, the family was broken, splintered, and scattered into new lives. My mother had remarried and was living with her new husband in the next county. My brother, in and out of juvenile detention his entire teenage years, was in a North Carolina state prison for marijuana possession, or something like that. To this day, we have never spoken about that closed chapter in his life. Like me, like so many of us, my brother has proudly remade his life.

But rather than push upstream, my floundering father had moved back in with his parents, back into his childhood bedroom in Greensboro, North Carolina, right next door to the little home he'd brought his bride to, and me his firstborn, just ten months after their wedding.

Perhaps my father had intended to rebuild his life from scratch, starting where it had all begun. Perhaps it is only true what everyone says, that the move back to my grandparents' home had been his attempt to hide out from loan sharks he thought he'd left behind in Roanoke. One cold February night shortly after midnight on a dark North Carolina highway, my father's white pickup truck mysteriously overturned and burst into flames. He was thirty-nine, just one week shy of his fortieth birthday. When the Red Cross alerted my commanding officer at Camp Lejeune, North Carolina, about my father's crash, I was by then a lance corporal, and engaged to Tom, who was an officer—an unlikely alliance, given Marine Corps regulations against fraternization.

Tom and I quickly received temporary orders that released us for several days, and drove to Greensboro. My father, according to the Red Cross, was still alive, but severely burned. Along the way, my mind played out what I might say to offer comfort. At some point, I began to cry, and Tom, who was driving, said, "I can't believe you're shedding a single tear for this guy." Tom had met my father once. The visit had been civil, but it was obvious the two men in my life were forged from different metal. At the end of that tension-filled weekend, my father had pulled me aside and whispered, "This man's not old enough for you, Honey." What? Tom was eight years older, I whispered back.

My father shook his head and climbed behind the wheel of his pickup. As he backed down the driveway, I wondered, have always wondered, what it was my father thought he understood, or misunderstood, about me.

Whatever his shortcomings—the drinking, the gambling, and the loan sharks—I couldn't accept my father as anything but sadly complicated and lost. Ironically, at the time in my life when I'd escaped my own bout with teenage alcoholism, joining the Marines for the discipline and sense of purpose I so desperately wanted and needed, and feeling then more in control than ever, my father was spinning recklessly further and further out of control.

The highway patrol officer who happened upon my father's overturned, burning truck and who pulled my father's charred body from the wreckage later concluded that my father must have fallen asleep behind the wheel or must have swerved to avoid someone, maybe a dog, in the middle of the road. Perhaps the cigarette perpetually dangling between my father's thick knuckles had ignited the fire. Any possibility sounded more appealing than what I knew we were all thinking: that my father had most likely been drunk when he lost control of his truck, or that the loan sharks had finally caught up to him. He survived two days in the burn ward of a Greensboro hospital. His last words were to my grandmother: "Mama, I'm sorry."

Whenever I think of my father, I picture him in mental snapshots divided between his pre-alcoholic and alcoholic stages. In the pre-alcoholic stage, my earlier childhood years, Dad was lean and handsome with gray eyes that were startling against his olive complexion. His hands were large, and I picture them most clearly gripped around the steering wheel with that cigarette between two fingers.

In the alcoholic stage, during my preteen years, he became

soft and paunchy, and brooded a lot. My parents were constantly worried about finances, though I didn't know this growing up. The money, I learned later, had been slipping between my father's fingers as easily as the straight bourbon down his throat.

On the good days, my father also laughed a lot. He would show up in the TV room with a football in his hands and ask, "Who's up for a game?" And he would put down the newspaper when I walked through the back door to whine about something my brother had done, and challenge me to rattle off as many numbers as I cared to. When I blurted out a string of complicated three- and four-digit numbers, he would glance up for a second as if waiting for the sum to materialize within the texture of the popcorn ceiling, and then he would smile when the numbers fell into place within his mind. I thought him a genius then. Looking back, I suspect he might have made up the answers, selling me even then on the notion of his genius.

On the good days, he was good to our mother, as well. One steamy summer night—in those years before central air—I had slipped from my bed after being awakened by a loud shuffling on the hardwood floors in our living room, and by my mother's giggling. The living room was nearly dark, the windows open, and in the hallway a refreshing draft caused by my open bedroom door. My parents were slow dancing to a Jerry Vale song. My mother was barefoot, wearing nothing but her full slip, the lace trim fluttering a bit from the breeze and from my father's dips and turns.

During those years, I had listened intently to my parents' discussions regarding presidential candidates—Humphrey, Nixon, and Wallace. In this, too, they could be united, so much so that when our elementary school held a mock election, I had convinced my entire class to vote for Nixon because my parents had agreed he was the best candidate for ending the Vietnam War. I knew little about the war. At nine, I thought I should want a copper bracelet like those the older girls wore, bracelets engraved with the names of Marines who had been declared missing or prisoners-of-war. To hold firmly to the name of a periled stranger symbolized a sordid combination of the romantic, dutiful, and tragic. But I never asked my mother for the money to buy a bracelet. By then, my mother had her own peril to fight. She began insisting the television be turned off during dinner, no doubt to block out war protests and race riots. After all, our home was under attack, often a war zone created by my father's unpredictable mood swings that were escalating into outbursts over the littlest of matters.

Evidence of his temper could be found in the holes his fists drove into the drywall and from the impressions in the wall of doorknobs from doors flung open too hard. And my kid brother, who had always been fond of throwing rocks, was now growing bored with throwing them into the creek or at a tree, and instead was throwing them at me. Once, while we had been playing a racing game to see who could make it first from the well in the backyard around the house to the front porch step, he got angry when he lost and threw a rock at me, striking my forehead. Mom nearly fainted when she saw the blood. She screamed for my brother to go to his room, and guided me into the house and to the kitchen, where she washed my face.

"It just won't stop bleeding," she said, though I had the sense she wasn't speaking to me. "It's busted open all right, but it's nothing serious." She rinsed the cloth under cold water and held it so hard against my forehead I was forced to lean against the counter to keep from falling backward. "Hold it right here," she said. I placed my hand over the cloth as hers pulled away. And then she stormed off to find my brother.

Another time, an afternoon during which my brother and I had somehow both forgotten our house keys and were waiting on the porch for one of our parents, he had tossed a small rock at me from the ground below the porch railing.

"Please quit," I said, and returned to the book I was reading. He answered with a shower of rocks from the driveway below the front porch, and then ran up the porch steps and pelted me at close range. I jumped from the rocker, pushed past him, and ran around the side of the house. Just as our father's car was pulling up the steep S-shaped driveway, I felt a sharp sting in the back of my head. I ran screaming toward my father, holding out my hands for him to see the blood, and then immediately regretted doing so when I was close enough to smell the alcohol on his breath. His already red, bloated face twisted into ugly rage. He bolted past me, unbuckling his belt along the way. My brother had disappeared inside the house. I could hear his footsteps running the hardwood staircase, and heard the slam of his bedroom door. My father, a charging bull, yanked the screen door nearly off its hinge and ran the steps to the second floor. I knew he wouldn't stop until he saw blood. I slumped on the bottom porch step and covered my ears to keep out my brother's screams and Dad's shouts. If our mother had been home, she, too, would have been screaming: "Stop, Jim—before you kill him!"

I never intervened on my brother's behalf. I wish I could have. I had been too afraid of turning my father's wrath from my brother to me.

★

In the interrogation room, the captain asked, "You're the Public Affairs officer for the New River Air Station, is that correct?"

"No, Ma'am." I was being technical, literal, perhaps even a bit coy.

The space between her eyes narrowed, squeezing out two military-straight parallel lines. "Okay, until you were relieved from duty two weeks ago. Is that correct?"

"Yes, Ma'am."

Her face relaxed, but I could still make out the shadows of those lines that seemed ready to spring forth when ordered. "Are you married?"

"Yes, Ma'am."

"Not divorced?" She was scribbling again on her legal pad, setting up her case for adultery.

"No, Ma'am."

She leaned over the desk and peered at the tape recorder. "Are you and your husband separated?"

"No."

"*No?*" There were those parallel lines again. "Are you sure about that?"

"Well, we weren't as of this morning, Ma'am." And this turn of curtness, or smugness, brought her full attention. My cheeks began to warm under a stare intent on locating a lie.

But it wasn't a lie. Just a few hours earlier and under a mental cloud of scheming to make a run for Canada, I had walked Tom and our six-year-old daughter to the car. He'd insisted that morning on driving Morgan to school. She was climbing into the back seat with her usual cheerfulness, and I was inhaling the sweet cloud of baby shampoo and minty toothpaste as I pulled the seat belt across her chest. "Will you meet me at the bus stop today?" she asked. This had been the same question every day throughout my two weeks on house arrest. Our first grader, after sampling life with a regular mom rather than with a Marine mom, had decided which of the two she preferred. It was easy to understand why Morgan liked being one of those kids who went home rather than to daycare after school; who wouldn't prefer a mom who was waiting for her at the bus stop, a mom who had an after-school snack prepared, a mom never too tired and grouchy to help with homework?

I must have smiled or given her something positive on which to pin her after-school hopes, for she had thrown her arms around my neck and planted with chapped lips on my mouth a hard, puckered kiss. How could I desert this child? How could I stay and endure the humiliation of a court-martial? I withdrew from the pocket of my bathrobe a tube of lip balm and swiped the ointment across her mouth. "Keep this," I whispered, pressing the tube into her palm and folding her fingers around it. I kissed her cheeks that were like fuzzy peaches.

Tom was standing behind me. I stood on my toes to kiss him, but I had kissed him too long. The kiss was a selfish one—a long, hard, selfish kiss to imprint into memory everything I could about him: the Old Spice aftershave, the high cheekbones inherited from his part-Cherokee mother, the hazel eyes. When I pulled away, his eyes narrowed into suspicion, as if he were reading my thoughts of fleeing to Canada. "Now you listen to me," he said, with a firm grip on my shoulders, "we will get through this."

All this, I could have offered as evidence to the captain and her tape recorder, but I said nothing, remembering my father's veteran sales advice to the poor novice encyclopedia salesman: "You have to know when to stop talking . . ."

The captain eventually broke the silence, and I felt the tiniest bit victorious. "Have you *ever* been separated, a marital separation?"

"Yes, Ma'am."

"When was that?"

"Last summer."

She inched the tape recorder toward me. "Why did you and your husband separate last summer?"

I glanced out the window, my gaze falling on the white, blooming dogwood I was noticing for the first time, thinking how I could have been an hour closer to Canada. By my calculations that morning on the drive through Jacksonville, North Carolina, passing the liquor stores and tattoo parlors, discount furniture businesses and used car dealerships, I had figured I could put at least three states in the rearview mirror before phone calls exhausted theories of whether or not I had been injured in a car crash on the way to the interrogation, or kidnapped by gypsies while pumping gas, or pistol whipped during a carjacking and wandering around with amnesia. A three-state head start would have been quite advantageous for a woman intent on deserting her military life, her husband, even her six-year-old daughter. I had also wanted to escape from the reporters who were calling our home nearly every day for two weeks. Reporters with promises to air my side of the story first in exchange for an exclusive. If reporters wanted headlines, I supposed a run to Canada would satisfy two possibilities: *Woman Marine Officer Missing*, replaced a few hours later with *Woman Marine Officer Flees*. Instead, I had turned around in the parking lot of an abandoned gas station, my tires crunching across gravel between two deserted islands of gas pumps; the sign on the door read: *We're closed. Please come again.*

The captain had taken to tapping her ink pen on the metal

desk. I wondered how the reverberations would play to those who later would be listening to the tape. In my head, I played out one answer and quickly discarded it for another. She was off track with her line of questioning. What had happened between Gen. John Hopkins and me had nothing to do with why Tom and I separated the summer before, though I suspect her orders were to see how tightly she could tie the two together.

★

The eighties was the decade of Reagan and Gorbachev. The fall of the Berlin Wall, the fairytale wedding of Diana to Prince Charles, the invasion into Grenada and Nicaragua. For women, it was also the decade of you-can-have-it-all. An entire generation of military women like me were determined—for better or for worse—to prove that the right Marine for the job could be a woman.

And so when I was facing the likelihood of a court-martial for conduct unbecoming an officer, I was also facing the reality that I was not only letting down my husband and my daughter, as soon as she learned of her mother's great shortcomings, but letting down all women in the Marines. In those days, we were women pushing women to ridiculous standards of self-sacrifice, demanding nothing less than perfection as Marines. Children, with their chronic earaches that forced daycare owners to call us away from our mission, were seen as liabilities by commanding officers—even, sadly, by us mothers who felt compelled to play the role of twenty-four-hour martyr. One misstep, one slightly visible pang of guilt or confusion about the priority of *God, Corps, and Country* reflected on us all. *See,* men jeered as we left to retrieve a sick child from daycare, *this is why women don't belong in the Corps.* But it wasn't just the men. Once, Morgan's daycare called, and my commanding officer—a woman lieutenant colonel—lashed out with, "Let that husband of yours go pick her up." Tom, as she very well knew, was a captain by then, and was even less expected, much less permitted, to leave his mission for a sick child than his wife, a sergeant.

For a ridiculous amount of time that morning before the interrogation, I had stared into my closet of military uniforms, trying to decide what one should wear to an interrogation. The winter alphas—the uniform with ribbons—seemed too formal; I'd save the alphas for the actual court-martial, if I didn't chicken out on the run to Canada. On the other hand, my usual winter uniform of slacks, pumps, khaki shirtwaist, and wool sweater with the patches on the shoulders and elbows seemed too casual. I finally settled on a long-sleeved shirtwaist that required a neck tab around the collar, my row of ribbons, a skirt instead of slacks, and pumps instead of the mannish and practical oxfords.

I wiggled into pantyhose and slipped on a skirt that was now too loose. Any other time in my life, I would have relished the weight loss, but this weight loss had been from a stress-induced inability to eat and not from the laxatives and diuretics I had relied on in my years as a Marine compelled to maintain the near impossible obligatory height-to-weight standard. Even the high-heeled pumps felt too large and foreign to my feet. During two weeks of house arrest, I had shuffled around the house in slippers, if I wore anything at all.

I pinned my red-and-gold officer's bars to the collar. When I slipped on the shirtwaist, it, too, felt loose. At least it was long enough to hide the top of my pantyhose that peeked above the waistband of the skirt.

In the bathroom, I leaned over the sink for a closer look into the vanity mirror. Dark half-moons under my eyes needed concealing. I dabbed on liquid foundation and rummaged listlessly past the brown eye shadow and past assorted compacts of blushes in the makeup case in search of black mascara. I pulled the wand from the mascara tube and found a lash stuck in the bristles. The lash was clumpy with black goo, and I blew it from the tip of my finger. A day or so earlier, Morgan had discovered a fallen eyelash on my cheek as we were seated at the kitchen table, poring over simple addition. She had held my eyelash in the palm of her hand. "Make a wish and blow, Mom." I had closed my eyes and blown the lash from her hand, wishing to end the madness I had brought into our lives.

For two weeks, I had been wandering our home on a sort of house arrest. My orders from the New River Air Station XO (executive officer) had been to "go home and stay there" until ordered otherwise. I did, and except for brief prison-like walks around the block for fresh air, I never left the house. What I remember most about those days was the pain on Tom's face, and my longing for that sensation that comes the second you realize you've awakened from a nightmare, or for the relief you feel on waking after having dozed at the wheel of your car, tires thumping along the safety squares of the center line.

Before leaving the house that morning of the interrogation, Tom was dressing for work. From a chair across our bedroom, I watched him walk to the dresser and peer into the mirror to ensure his rank insignia were properly pinned in place, and when he glanced at me through the mirror, I looked away, afraid he would read in my expression, desertion. He released a heavy sigh and slumped onto the edge of a chair, where he laced his boots and bloused his trousers.

I stood, and was untying the sash around the waist of my bathrobe when he said, "I'll take Morgan to school this morning." It was more an order than an offer. He was standing again before the dresser, this time staring at my reflection in the mirror and looking years older than thirty-four. I had done that to him.

I cinched the robe and shuffled toward the kitchen, where Morgan was finishing her cereal.

After they left, I nervously puttered around the house in my bathrobe and slippers, mentally carving in the memories of this life should I have the strength—or was it cowardice?—to run to Canada. I straightened Morgan's childish attempt at bed-making. I looked in her closet, in her toy chest, in her dresser for something and nothing in particular. On top of her dresser was a framed photograph of the three of us, taken several years earlier when Tom and I had been stationed in California. They, too, had been difficult years. I had been relentless in my efforts to prove myself in this man's world, and this had caused problems in our marriage. Tom was never able to understand why I couldn't be satisfied with our life: Why I wasn't satisfied with being the wife of an officer and the mother of a beautiful child. Why I volunteered for military missions that took me weeks, sometimes months, away from our family. Years after we succumbed to a divorce came the painful realization that perhaps I *had* fought too hard to let Tom, any man, keep me from doing the job for which I'd been trained. The deepest secret of all was that living a life full of purpose and achievement—a life for me and me alone—ensured sobriety. I was afraid of those stagnant waters: afraid that if I ever stopped pushing upstream, despite getting knocked around by others, I'd eventually drown in a cesspool of my own making.

The captain was still waiting for an answer about why Tom and I had separated that summer. She turned her head toward the window, and in profile, I had a singular perspective of her that could make you wonder whether there even was a second eye, a second ear, a second cheek, a second nostril.

She was married. I knew this, not because of the band around her ring finger, but because her husband, a chief warrant officer, found plenty of excuses to show up at my Public Affairs office. He would close the door and unleash a torrent of gripes about how poorly he thought our CO was running the air station. He hadn't been the only staff officer to use my office as a venue for airing frustration about the CO. Maybe I was a good listener. Maybe *Public Affairs* on my door suggested I couldn't be shocked by anything they told me. Maybe because I was the only woman on the CO's staff . . .

The captain tapped her pen again on the metal desk. "Answer the question, please. Why did you and your husband separate last summer?" The tapping stopped and her pen hovered above the desk.

"I'd prefer to keep the personal details of my marriage private, Ma'am."

She jotted something onto the legal pad. "You realize," she said, not looking up, "that this is an investigation . . . that you're facing a violation of Article 32 under the Uniform Code of Military Justice for conduct unbecoming an officer. You're facing a court-martial. Things might go easier for you if you cooperate." The captain was staring at my left hand, my wedding ring. She cleared her throat.

"Maybe it would help, Ma'am," I said, stalling, "if someone would finally tell me the nature behind the charge. In two weeks, no one has *officially* told me anything."

Her legs had been crossed at the knees and now she was unfolding them and crossing them again, opposite leg over the other. "Let me ask the questions, Warrant Officer."

It wasn't entirely true that I didn't know the nature behind the charge, but I wanted someone to end the madness by confirming it. My only clue had come from the telephone conversation with the major in charge of Public Affairs at Cherry Point, the air station located forty miles northeast of Jacksonville. I'd called him from home the day I was fired.

"This is big," he had said.

"What could I possibly have done?" The question had been

uttered as much to the major on the other end of the telephone line as to Tom, who, having rushed home when I called with the news of being fired, was now sitting on the edge of a chair across the bedroom from me. From where I sat on the edge of our bed, he appeared dressed for battle in his combat boots and camouflage uniform. In our years together, we had consoled each other through two miscarriages, had survived a number of military separations and the loss of a daughter in childbirth, had even survived a three-month marital split the summer before.

"I've called all my contacts down there," the major added. "Everyone's afraid to talk about it. Word is, no one's allowed to talk to you. Not even legal. You'll have to find a civilian attorney. I'm hearing your CO is behind this."

My CO was a colonel who had flown helicopter combat missions in Vietnam. He looked prematurely aged from all he had seen and done there. Unless he was throwing back shots at the O Club, or holding Kangaroo Court where the mistakes of his staff were retold for jeering, he rarely smiled. Twice he had even called my office and breathed heavily into the phone, *I'm watching you . . . I know what you're doing*, and hung up.

I should have reported the harassment and would have if not for a conversation in 1985 with the general in charge of Public Affairs in DC. The general had been making his sweep through East Coast offices and stopped at my office two weeks after my CO assumed command of the air station. The general, also a pilot once, described behind closed doors his relationship with my CO. I learned the two men had flown helicopter missions together over Vietnam.

"I'm worried about you," the general admitted. "I want you to know I'll be watching for the fitness reports he writes about your performance down here."

I described my first awkward meeting with the CO, the week

before, the colonel having ordered each of his staff officers into his office for one-on-one introductions. When my turn had come, I stood at attention before his desk and felt his eyes size me from head to toe, and back again. When his head dipped over his desk, I let my eyes follow. He was leaning over my SRB, my service record book, and flipping through pages. He hovered over a page.

"Two Navy Achievements medals?" he said, his head still over the page.

"Yes, Sir."

He flipped the page and paused again. "Rifle expert?"

"Yes, Sir."

"Sharpshooter with your .45 and .38?"

"Yes, Sir."

He closed the SRB and sat in his chair. "Two things you need to know. I don't like warrant officers and I especially don't like women in the Marine Corps. That's two strikes against you already."

I'm not sure which surprised me most, his open misogyny or his dislike of warrant officers. After all, warrant officers are former enlisted Marines who have proven themselves, at least to a highly selective board of senior officers, as tested leaders and as experts in their field. Since enlisted Marines lavish respect on a warrant officer and offer it only dutifully to an inexperienced second lieutenant, perhaps somewhere in the colonel's history he was remembering a moment when, as a young lieutenant in Vietnam, he had been slighted.

Before dismissing me, he asked, "Is there anything you'd like to say?"

I was expected, of course, to say no.

"Yes, Sir."

His salty eyebrows lifted above the rims of his wire frames.

"I'd like to say that, as the colonel's Public Affairs officer, I expect to be considered first string—Sir."

The colonel stiffened, then slowly rose to his feet. He held out my SRB. When I reached for it, I saw he was smiling.

"I'll keep that in mind," the colonel said, taking his time to release the record book in that way some men have of lingering too long with a handshake, or with eye contact. "You're dismissed, *Warrant* Officer."

The general, on hearing the recapping of this experience, had shaken his head. "If things get bad down there, you call me." Unfortunately, by the time things reached their worst, the general had retired.

The major from Cherry Point assured me he wouldn't quit until he got an answer for why I had been fired. "Let me call Headquarters Marine Corps," he said. "Someone there will apply pressure to find out what all this craziness is about. Don't worry. We'll get to the bottom of it."

I thanked him, set the receiver into the cradle, and jumped when it rang back. I immediately recognized the voice on the other end: a reporter from the *Jacksonville Daily News*. I used to imagine him driving around in his car, straining to make out the garbled codes from his police scanner. He had been the first to call me eight months earlier when one of the air station's CH-46 helicopters crashed off the coast during a training exercise, killing all nineteen on board. During the Oliver North trial, he was the first to call for permission to come aboard the air station and interview Marines about their feelings on the Iran-Contra Affair. He was the first to call for a military reaction to the Challenger shuttle launch disaster.

"Tracy," he said, "I just heard something's going down at the air station that involves you . . . let me get your side of the story out there first."

"Thanks, Rick, but I'll have to get back to you."

I looked over at Tom, who was leaning forward in the chair across the room, his arms on his legs. "I can't believe this is happening," I said. "I should be crying or screaming or something, but I feel numb."

"You're in shock," he said. "This is all too unbelievable."

The phone rang again. This time it was the major from Cherry Point, and I sensed he was being careful now about the words he chose. "Do you know a general? Over at Lejeune?"

My expression must have deceived me. Tom leaped from the chair to stand beside me. His hand on my shoulder felt clumsy and heavy. I stammered into the phone. "May I call you back, Major?"

In the interrogation room, the captain was staring out the window for the first time that morning. "I realize these questions about your marriage must be uncomfortable. You're trying to protect your husband, aren't you?" She looked back at me.

The question lingered in the room on the hum of a whirring cassette tape. *No,* I could have answered quickly enough. Tom needed no protection. My husband knew the truth, now: a confession that hadn't come easy. But he had been forgiving, even reassuring that we could get past this. After all, we had been separated at the time of my affair, not that this mattered to the Corps. According to regulations, an intimate relationship prior to a final divorce decree was adultery.

No, the one who needed my protection now was Gen. John Hopkins.

★

I was eleven the first time I fell in love with a general.

On a Thursday night in 1970, a night when my brother was in the hospital recovering from a hernia operation and my mother was staying the night with him, my father took me to see the movie he said everyone was talking about.

Here's how I remember it. George C. Scott as General Patton in Army uniform steps onto the stage. Salutes. In the background, an enormous American flag. We are watching him hold the salute through a trumpet call for reveille. The camera cuts to an ivory-handled pistol, the helmet with four stars, a baton, rows of medals, that pinky ring. My father's munching popcorn, drinking a Coke.

Patton, or rather Scott as Patton, is addressing a class of recruits who would soon leave to join the fight against the Nazis. We never see the recruits, but sitting there in the dark theater next to my father, I felt strangely like one of them: the good girl who followed the rules to keep from sparking war within her family.

At the beginning of *Patton*, Scott delivers his famous monologue about sacrifice and bravery. My father was shaking the tub of popcorn at me, and as I reached for another buttery handful, on the screen General Patton began swearing in that voice that reminded me of tires grinding along a gravel driveway, and I pulled my hand back. *You win a war by letting some* other *poor bastard die for his country* . . . When the general finished, I reached for more popcorn and glanced up at my father. Underneath the fragments of moving shadows that played across his face was an odd and unfamiliar expression. I suddenly had the feeling I was sitting next to a stranger, helping myself to his popcorn.

What about war and killing and sacrifice and honor among men did my father wish to share with me? In the dark theater that night watching *Patton*, my father felt too far away from the life that included my mother, brother, and me. He had locked himself inside a private chamber within his mind. What was he learning there? What was he questioning? *Under life's most difficult conditions, would I? Could I?* What, retreat? Desert? Hold your ground? Be brave? Jump on the grenade to save the others?

Or maybe I'm wrong. Maybe all these thoughts were only firing into me.

The same year my father had taken me to see *Patton*, his sales started slipping. He was coming home later in the evenings, and when he did make it for dinner, the atmosphere around the table was as thick as one of my mother's overcooked pork chops.

One night, he slammed his knife onto the table, causing all of us to jump. He shouted to my mother across the table that I was chewing too loudly. I could feel the lump rising like yeast in my throat. I couldn't remember the last time my father had criticized me. I was the good kid: the one who chose to play the clarinet to please him rather than the piano to please my mother, and myself; the one who brought home straight As; the one who stayed out of trouble. My brother was staring wide-eyed at his dinner plate as if he were waiting for a hole to magically open there between the mashed potatoes and English peas for him to crawl down into. A glance at my mother revealed her eyes were filling with tears. She lowered her head, and I felt betrayed.

My father, however, had resumed his eating, slicing up a pork chop with a knife that angrily raked against the plate while my brother and mother picked at their food. My brother lifted his glass of milk, glanced at me, and quickly diverted his glance, as if he thought by looking at me, he, too, might be found guilty of something. I was too fearful to try another bite, and stared down at the plate. My father apparently noticed I had stopped eating and, misreading my fear as martyrdom, dropped his fork onto his plate and angrily pushed his chair from the table. After he stormed from the room, I looked at the long scratch in the linoleum. A permanent scar.

A few hours later that evening, after my father stormed out the front door, someone from PET called and spoke to my mother. No, he wasn't home, she said in a shaky voice. No, she didn't know when he'd be home. I detected the concern in her voice.

Later, their argument woke me.

"You can't keep doing this, Jim."

"I'll do any goddam thing I want!"

"If you won't think of yourself or me, then think of the children."

The loosely confederated threads holding my family together were unraveling. On Friday nights, I was a cheerleader for the Cloverdale Cougars' basketball team. The games were held at the local high school. Dad always drove me to and from the games, which I recall as a sordid combination of fun and fright.

Parents crowded into bleachers while the boys warmed up on the court, practicing layups and free throws, their shoes squeaking on the glossy court floor. In the corners of the gymnasium, a handful of parents sold sodas and boxes of popcorn to raise money for the next year's basketball uniforms.

My mother never came to a game, because my father insisted on coming to all of them. Up on the last bleacher with his back against the wall, my father sat, drunk. "C'mon ref, what kind of call is that? What's the matter, lose your glasses?"

"Sit down, Mister!" a few parents would yell.

I sat on the bottom bleacher with the other cheerleaders, my back to him, to everyone, and cheered for rebounds and a stronger defense and *Make that shot, Team, make that shot!*

When my father got too personal in his shouts, the ref would toss him out of a game and charge our team with a technical foul. Parents would boo, and the coach would plead with the ref. I pretended not to know the man who huffed down the bleachers, who crossed middle court screaming obscenities, who waited for me in the parking lot without apologies on the quiet ride home.

Finally, one night from the back seat, I heard a voice like mine ask, *Dad, why do you drink when you promised us you would quit?* My father's hands tightened around the steering wheel until I thought the skin between his knuckles would split open. Between two fingers, a cigarette wavered. As a child, I had always worried his cigarettes would break, fall into his lap, and burn him to death.

Dad rolled down the window and I shivered. Red sparks from the cigarette fluttered past my window. "Let me make this clear," he yelled above the roar of wind as he rolled up the window. As the window reached closure, the road noise seemed vacuumed away, leaving behind a second of silence that was far more deafening. "I can drink and quit drinking anytime I want!" His fingers had snapped on *anytime.*

"Well," I said, through chattering teeth, "could you quit on Friday nights then?"

At first my father had been speechless. Then a strange gurgling rose from deep within his throat, from a place even deeper than that, from someplace guttural, from the someplace before me, from the someplace of his boyhood. It was laughter.

★

Years later, the night I decided to tell my mother I had joined the Marines, she was washing the last dinner plate and rinsing both sides under running hot water. The extra heat was converting the tiny kitchen of our mobile home into a sauna. She set the plate face down onto the drain board for me to dry, and then her hand disappeared into the soapy sink to pull the plug. The suds made a swirling, immaculate exit.

Several weeks earlier, I had met first with Army recruiters at the military recruiting offices in downtown Roanoke. In some silly girlish way, I suppose I had been expecting to meet a General Patton, and I hadn't. Neither did the recruiters resemble what I had pictured as Patton's recruits. These men had bellies that spilled over their belts. The buttons on their shirts appeared strained under the pressure.

Next door to the Army's office was the Navy's. The Navy recruiter was a man with salty hair and saltier breath. He pointed to a chair beside his desk, asked me questions about how long I had been out of high school and about what hobbies I had. I told him I liked dogs and had grown up around dog shows. When I told him I knew a little about dog obedience training, his face brightened. He flipped through a fat spiral notebook for information on how to become a Military Police dog handler. All this appealed to me until he said there was a six-month waiting list for women.

I left the Navy's office and walked the narrow hallway to the Air Force office. These recruiters, three men, were different, but I wasn't sure how, except that they carried themselves in a casual way and their blue pants and lighter-blue shirts with the open collars reminded me more of post office workers or ticket agents for an airline company. By now, the idea of becoming a dog handler with Military Police was wearing well on me, and the Air Force recruiter confirmed he could sign me up for Military Police, if only I could wait six months for an opening to boot camp.

Defeated, I headed for the exit. Against a wall near the entrance leaned a man in navy-blue trousers with scarlet stripes down the outer sides of each trouser leg. His hair was shaved close to the scalp, and he was wearing a fitted khaki short-sleeve shirt with a mountain of stripes on his sleeves and rows of ribbons on his chest, a tie, and the shiniest black shoes I'd ever seen.

"Young lady, you haven't checked out the Marines."

"They have women in the Marines?"

He smiled and motioned toward his office. "Let me show you a film."

The Marine staff sergeant was the first recruiter that day to shake my hand and to pull out a chair. He switched on a small television, and I watched a short film about the Marines. I saw young men and women, my age, in real jobs: banking, clerical, military police, truck driving, and aircraft maintenance. Women in smart-fitting uniforms looked as if they had found a purpose to their lives.

"Where do I sign?" I asked at the end of the movie.

He rolled his eyes and leaned back in his chair. "So, you're running from the police, right?"

"No!"

"Ever been arrested?"

"No."

"Graduate from high school?"

"Of course."

He leaned forward and rested his forearms on the desk. His hands formed a steeple.

"Ever done drugs?"

"No." I made the assumption he was talking about narcotics and not beer or wine, for by then I was battling my own drinking problem and fearful I was becoming my father.

"How soon could you be ready to go?"

"Tomorrow?"

He laughed, and then from a desk drawer, he withdrew a wad of forms that fell with a thud on the desk.

In a back room, I completed and passed a preliminary exam, except for the spatial portion for which I was supposed to mentally fold boxes along their dotted and bent lines to match up with one of the answers. I couldn't visualize a single correct answer. The recruiter said he would teach me how to *fold those little boxes* before taking the real test in Richmond. But in the end, after weeks of failing to mentally fold boxes and resigned to defeat, the recruiter eventually gave me the answers to the test, claiming, "No one who wants to be a Marine as bad as you should be kept out of the Corps over a few stupid boxes." And that was that. I spent the next ten years proving I belonged in the Marines as much as anyone else, despite the fact I'd had to cheat my way in.

Back in the tiny kitchen of our mobile home, I was still struggling with how to tell my mother I had joined the Marines. She was wringing out the dishcloth for her nightly ritual of wiping down the kitchen: countertops, stove top, dinette table, the faces of wood cabinets, and the refrigerator. When she was finished, she rinsed the cloth and draped it over the stainless steel faucet, glancing out the window above the sink, out over the dry, summer acres toward the fence gate, where her horse, Baron, was waiting for his supper of oats and grain, his head bobbing over barbed wire, tail flicking away the flies. He nuzzled against a fence post, stamped a foot in the dirt like an impatient toddler. My mother sighed. Here, on five acres in a valley ringed by the purple Appalachian Mountains, my mother had finally found her paradise.

Paradise hadn't come easy. She had married my father at eighteen, given birth to me ten months later, and to my brother eighteen months afterward.

The night my parents decided to divorce, they had called upstairs for us to join them in the living room. My brother and I had been in our bedrooms, working on homework, and when we met at the top of the stairs, my brother's eyebrows had lifted into a question I didn't need to answer: this was it; we both felt it. It was January 1972, a week after my thirteenth birthday, a week since the Redskins' Super Bowl loss to the Miami Dolphins. My father had waited his entire life to see his team in the Super Bowl, and the Redskins' quarterback, Billy Kilmer, had killed all chances of a victory, as my father saw it. He had screamed at the television, "Put in Jurgensen, you goddam idiots!"

From the kitchen, where she had been preparing dinner, my mother called out, "Jim, the children!"

My father had lifted the bowl of onion dip from the coffee table and hurled a precision pass—in fact, the best we had seen all day—toward the kitchen, narrowly missing my mother's head, to splat across the front of the refrigerator. That was the last time my mother would pick up the pieces of her marriage.

Ironically, I heard myself pleading for them to find a way to make it work. They were grown-ups, I said. Grown-ups were supposed to know how to fix things. My father glanced at my mother, who was now looking wounded, as if I had betrayed her. In all honesty, I hadn't seen the things she and my brother had seen. But neither had they seen my father tossed from a basketball game or driving with a speedometer needle inching past ninety. All this, I had kept to myself. Protecting him. Protecting all of us. If I could live with public humiliation, why couldn't they?

As our parents explained divorce and new living arrangements that had us kids going with Mom, and Dad staying behind in our old home, I wondered who, if not us, would save Dad from himself.

We moved to a small duplex, where my mother and I shared a bedroom. My father eventually moved into an apartment with another company salesman. Months went by without word from him. Sometimes we would hear frightening things, such as how he owed money to the wrong people. Other times, the news was good: he was sober and back on the job.

On the first Christmas Eve since the family's separation, my mother, brother, and I were watching television. Jimmy Stewart was giving life a second go in *It's a Wonderful Life*, the part where Jimmy's character discovers that if he hadn't stayed behind to manage the family's savings and loan, his brother wouldn't have been in the right place to save all those troops. Suddenly, the sound of splintering glass made the three of us jump to our feet. The front door panes were crashing to the floor. My father kicked in the door, crunched across a carpeting of glass shards, and shouted something about it being Christmas and how family should always be together at Christmas. Blood splattered across the white walls, and the armload of gifts he had tucked under his arm when he crashed through the door was falling into a heap on the floor.

"Please get out, Jim! Think of the children."

My mother ran to the telephone. My father pulled the phone from her hands and threw it across the room. My brother skirted undetected past both of them and out the back door. We discovered afterward he had run barefoot through the snow to the neighbors for help.

I picked up each of my father's gifts and hurled them at him.

"Get out!" I screamed. "You're drunk! Don't ever come back like this!"

This time, there would be no laughter. My father broke into guttural sobs and stumbled for the door.

My mother had worked two jobs to support us. During days, she was an executive secretary for a trucking company. Shortly after five, she dashed through the front door, shouting questions about our day at school and orders about not going outside when she wasn't home and directions on how to cook whatever she had left thawing in the sink all day, while she quick-changed into a black-and-white waitress uniform for work at the Holiday Inn until sometime after midnight.

On days she thawed fish for me to cook, I waited until the gravel settled in the driveway, and then I tossed the fish, package and all, into the woods behind the duplex. My brother and I walked down the street to the hamburger grill on the corner, where I bought supper with the money I earned from babysitting jobs. After dinner, we would head to the empty lot a block from the duplex, where all the neighborhood kids gathered after supper to play baseball until dark.

And then, in the way life has of seeming to change overnight, I was a senior in high school, sitting in the guidance counselor's office, listening to this woman lecture me about how I needed Algebra II to get into college, when it dawned on me that this woman was the first to ever mention the idea: of me, in college.

Neither of my parents had attended college, unless you count that one semester my father did at Elon College. I remember my grandmother describing how she had saved up for his suitcase, squirreling away money from the grocery budget, and how my father had brought his clothes home every weekend in that suitcase for washing, and on Sunday, my grandmother had repacked the suitcase for his return to Elon. But he hadn't wanted college. College had been his parents' dream for him. My father was dreaming about the girl he left behind each week, my mother. And so after a few weekends of this coming and going, of washing and drying and ironing, my father had set the suitcase in the closet of his childhood bedroom and didn't take it out until six months later to pack for a honeymoon.

How could I tell the guidance counselor I didn't come from the kind of family that talked about and planned for college? She was cheerily spreading her assortment of colored brochures across her desk, reminding me of the encyclopedia salesman all those years ago in our living room. She was trying to sell me on choices with her brochures of ivy-covered buildings and manicured walkways and kids about my age, except they were wearing smiles and nicer clothing. I could tell from her enthusiasm she believed in her product, higher education, as much as the encyclopedia salesman had believed in his. But if either of my parents had been saving for college, or even a suitcase, I figured they would have mentioned it by now. And since no one had ever mentioned me and college in the same breath, I had assumed I wasn't going. Couldn't go. I hadn't even signed up for the entrance exams. But here was the guidance counselor with the mousy-brown hair and wire eyeglass frames telling me that if I would only turn my life into a living hell during senior year with Algebra II, my reward would be college.

"I think I'll pass."

"Pass?" She settled back in her chair, and a single eyebrow lifted. "Pass on what, Tracy? Life? Where will this leave you? What is your plan?"

And that was when it hit me. I had no plan. I had no plan for life after high school. As if a life after high school had never seemed possible, until now.

There was a second sigh in Paradise. Back in the kitchen of our mobile home, in one hand my mother held the broom and in the other the dustpan. I had been dragging out the chore of drying the dishes, delaying the announcement I had joined the Marines, delaying whatever reaction the news would draw. I couldn't leave news like this to the last minute, could I? Not say anything until the night before I left for boot camp at Parris Island? Not say, *Good-bye?* A hug, maybe? A chance to hear, *I love you?* A chance to say it again after all these years?

I dried the plate, stashed it in the cabinet, and took the dustpan. Between my feet, she dabbed the broom, standing back, waiting for me to clear the way. Why was I always in her way? I stepped over to carpet, and she rooted for crumbs in the corners under cabinets as if I had been hiding them all along.

We hadn't spoken through dinner that evening. Since the divorce five years earlier, nothing felt worth the hassle words could cause us. I suppose my mother and I were not unlike most mothers and daughters. If my stepfather, a long-distance trucker, had been home that evening, his cheeriness would have made it easier for the two of us to combine words with food.

I bent down with the dustpan. She swept and I accommodated her moves. The broom smelled like the haystacks in our barn. Sweet, promising. I had always loved the smell of hay. Loved cutting away the twine, anticipating the separation within the bundle, the excitement of finding dry pressed clovers among the stalks, someone's missed lucky clovers my gain, and it was during these times in the barn, the days leading up to the announcement, that I began to doubt my decision to join the Marines.

My mother was probably wondering as she swept crumbs into the dustpan when, no if, I would ever leave home; after all, hadn't graduation been three whole months earlier? And so, when I finally uttered the words that night about leaving home in a few weeks, about joining the military—*The Marines, for God's sake?*—my body began to slowly disconnect from the dustpan, withdraw from the kitchen, as if to free itself to slide through the open window above the sink where moments earlier the suds had swirled around and around toward the drain, and then I felt myself floating out over the fields beyond our fence line, past the giant oak at the edge of the driveway, and toward places I hadn't yet been able to picture, until my mother recaptured me with a smile. She was prettiest when she smiled. And I loved her most in those rare moments when the smile was turned upon me. She had grown up the oldest of five, and since her mother's death from cancer a few years earlier, had become the matriarch of a family that included two brothers whose ages were within a year of her children's.

"I wanted to join the military," she said, the smile slowly fading, "but Mother always believed nice girls didn't." My mother and her mother shared a common definition of nice: nice girls remained virgins until married.

She was staring at the black onyx ring on my left hand. If she had asked to see it, I would have slipped it from my finger, dropped it into her palm. I would have smiled as she read the inscription inside the band, *summer of '77*. I might have even told the truth if she had asked how a girl like me, who could barely afford gas for her car for the long ride from the country to her job in town at the veterinary clinic, could have saved enough for expensive jewelry. My mother wanted to ask about the ring. Everything in her face said so, but she didn't ask.

So I thought, why ruin it for her? Why confirm she hasn't

raised a nice girl? She didn't need to know her daughter was running around town with a married man, or that her daughter had become an alcoholic, drinking her way through senior year, and she didn't need to know about the night the band director caught her daughter drunk and lectured her with, *You're a born leader, why are you doing this to yourself?*

No, my mother didn't need to hear all this the night I told her about joining the Marines. She didn't want to hear that her daughter had become a drunk anymore than she wanted to know that her daughter had been sneaking into and out of cheap hotels with a married man who had given her a black onyx ring, or for that matter, that her daughter had been driving at night through Roanoke's peach orchards on Highway 604, dodging trees, or that her daughter was meeting *him* among the peach groves: peach pits pressing into her daughter's kidneys, the rotting smell of something too old on her skin and in her hair, the stars winking through the swaying branches, while his face slightly off center of hers tried too hard to fill an empty well.

But weeks later, in a crowded room in downtown Richmond, filled with Marines in uniform and teenagers in bell-bottoms, teenagers who looked nothing like me and everything like me, I uttered an oath to *support and defend the Constitution of the United States of America against all enemies foreign and domestic,* and I promised myself I could be better. I *would* be better.

★

The next day was the longest day of my life.

It was October 25, 1977, the start to eight weeks of boot camp at Parris Island near the coastal town of Beaufort, South Carolina. The flight from Richmond to Charleston was my first time on an airplane. I hadn't been nervous, nor had I felt the moment particularly auspicious. I was numb, maybe in shock.

The bus transporting us from the Charleston airport to the recruit depot was filled with quiet teenagers. No one was playing cards or singing about the number of beers on the wall or sharing their stories about enlisting or whom they'd left behind. It was the middle of the night, and I heard no one utter a sound as we whizzed closer to Parris Island, passing one small rural town after another and the dimmed lights of fast-food chain restaurants, the bus occasionally lit up by a row of unexpected streetlamps.

When the driver finally brought the bus to a halt and opened the door, we were assaulted by the fishy odor of swamp water. About a third of Parris Island's eight thousand or so acres are unusable marshland, and full of alligators.

It's true, you know—that iconic image of teenagers stumbling off a bus under the shouts of drill instructors.

Something like fear lurched in my stomach as I made my way from the middle of the bus and down the steps to claim a pair of yellow painted footprints on the pavement. A drill instructor with a deep voice was shouting that we were to stand at the position of attention. I knew what this meant from my years in the high school band. I stood as still as possible, trying not to flinch at the bite of what I'd later discover were sand fleas. "Don't move, don't you dare move," a drill instructor barked at the woman in front of me, who made the rookie mistake of swatting at the buggers.

I have always said the Marines must ship in sand fleas to Parris Island just to teach discipline. The wait for the others to disembark the bus seemed an eternity. Every time a sand flea crawled near the inside corners of my eyes, I closed them and sent up a silent prayer against the bites on my ear lobes, the back of my neck, and wrists.

We were eventually divided by sex, and women drill instructors led us to another room, where we sat at long tables and completed paperwork. Finally, we were ushered to the barracks, which was an enormous room filled with rows and rows of racks in bunk-bed manner. I dropped my suitcase beside a bottom rack and lay down. For a minute.

Like a nuclear flash, light flooded the barracks, and the room came alive under the barking orders of several women drill instructors. "Reveille, reveille—in front of your racks," they shouted. "At the position of attention." The drill instructors strode up and down the center aisle and banged on the bottom of brown metal trash cans. My heart was pounding in my ears.

I stood quietly at attention beside a curly redhead, Wheeler, who I was to learn later had grown up on her family's dairy farm in Appleton, Wisconsin. When she thought it safe, she turned and smiled. I don't remember smiling back. What I do remember is what I was thinking then and the rest of the day: What had been so bad, after all, about living with my mother? I wanted to go home. I wanted to shout, "Wait, this is all a big mistake—I don't belong here."

But I did belong there. Within days, I was appointed squad leader because I was apparently the only one who could march in a straight line—thanks to all those hours of band practice. I soaked up the military history classes that described Marine heroes such as Chesty Puller and the distinguished battles of Belleau Wood, where the Germans nicknamed Marines Devil Dogs. In image classes, I learned how to hold my gloves, to carry my purse over my left forearm, and to coordinate the color of my lipstick with the color of the scarlet rope cord on our headgear.

When we weren't in classes, we were marching or running, and the confinement eventually got to some of us. Rumors of desertion floated through the barracks. I was too exhausted to think of any activity that involved movement. I hardly had the strength to write a letter home, and didn't write but two letters in eight weeks. The boyfriend—the married lover—was so worried by week six that he called headquarters at Parris Island and demanded proof that I was safe. The night that Staff Sergeant Scott called me to the office for a phone call, I was spit shining my shoes. I set down the soiled rag and scurried to my feet. When I heard his voice, I hung up. "Everything okay?" Scott asked in a tone of concern that nearly caused me to drop to my knees out of gratitude.

"Ma'am, the private is fine, Ma'am," I said, and hurried back to the barracks.

About three weeks in, three girls huddled on the floor in the middle of two bunks. They whispered actual plans about desertion the next night. But the next night, and every night for a week, after lights out and after the platoon's singing of "The Lord's Prayer," Sergeant Koile or Crews would shout into the barrel of darkness, "Don't even think about deserting . . . you'll never survive the alligators."

Two days before Christmas, we graduated from boot camp. The day was so cold that the ceremony, for the sake of our families, had been moved inside a base gymnasium where our platoon had run circles around the squeaky floor until I felt as trapped and hopeless as a gerbil on a wheel.

On the creaky wooden bleachers were rows of unfamiliar faces of people dressed in drab, shapeless winter clothing. I hadn't spotted my father or grandparents until after our platoon was marched in and given an about-face. Huddled inside her camel-colored coat was my grandmother. She sat between my father and grandfather, who were wearing heavy windbreaker jackets. Both men had their hands in their pockets, something no Marine is ever allowed to do, nor chew gum in uniform, or carry any object in any hand other than the left—leaving the right always free for snappy salutes. All this I remember trying to mentally hang onto as I stood stoic and tall in formation, as if fearful I would immediately forget everything when engulfed by the oncoming wave of civilian influence.

I couldn't help but feel sorry for how uncomfortable and out of place everyone in the bleachers appeared, including my father and grandparents. My parents' divorce had been final a year after the ugly Christmas Eve scene during which my father had crashed through the front door. But that wasn't why my mother hadn't come to graduation; she was at home in Roanoke, recovering from severe injuries she had suffered when her car slid on ice and crashed into the side of a mountain. My brother had been in and out of the juvenile court system and, at sixteen, was still living in a halfway house for troubled teens.

From my position in the third row of our platoon I stood firmly at attention and let my eyes shift left to right down the two rows of women ahead of me, suppressing a giggle for how, in our tailored uniforms, we'd been transformed into a platoon of perfectly shaped and aligned hourglasses.

From his seat in the bleachers, my father was smiling and

pointing toward the platoon, and I knew this meant he had located his hourglass daughter. My grandparents were trying to follow the imaginary line that extended from my father's fingertip to me. My grandmother reached into her purse, took out her eyeglass case, and situated her glasses over her nose. My father pointed again and she followed his long arm and beyond, but shook her head and removed the glasses. My grandfather, however, was smiling.

At the conclusion of the ceremony, my father and grandparents were straining to see over and around the tops of young women in Marine headgear. I waved and my father waved back. He navigated my grandmother by the elbow through an olive-green sea that quickly parted into rivulets of reuniting families.

My grandmother was the first to hug me. She screamed, "You're too thin!" And, "I was afraid we wouldn't find you, you're all dressed alike."

My father laughed. "I knew her the minute she walked in . . . I'd know that walk of hers anywhere."

And so, despite how hard I had worked for eight weeks to blend in, my father's comment was one of the first hints for how little control I had over my body. For years afterward, I fought my body's weaknesses with hundreds of push-ups and miles of running. I fought its femininity by wearing girdles and bras too tight for my chest.

In the military world, and sober for the first time in years, I found I was better about a number of things. For one, I was feeling an acute awareness about everything, myself and my surroundings. Life had never been as clear. It was as if I had somehow flipped a switch to activate all five senses at once. And *home* was merely that place where my mother lived.

After boot camp, I worked for the local recruiting office for ten days, successfully recruiting two women. Then, I left for Camp

Lejeune the day after an ice storm blanketed Roanoke. From my bedroom, where I was packing suitcases, I heard the snap of tree limbs falling victim to the weight of ice. The front steps were covered with a sheet of ice so thick I had had to slide my suitcases to the bottom of the porch and wiggle down on my backside. The short path to the car was a slippery slope. My mother sat on the sofa, watching. "Isn't there someone you can call and explain you can't possibly leave here until the highways are safe?"

I laughed. "Mom, it just doesn't work that way. Short of death, there is no excuse for an unauthorized absence." My mother had lost control of me since the divorce, and from the expression on her face I believe I read a sense of envy: someone or something had been more successful than she at exercising control over her daughter. I almost felt sorry for her.

I was headed out the door with another suitcase. "But tomorrow's your birthday," she said. I had howled over that one, letting the storm door crash behind me.

The next day, on my nineteenth birthday, I waited to leave home as late as I thought I could. I told my mother I was waiting for the rising temperatures to thaw the roads. Truth is, I was afraid to leave. I had never driven more than two hours by myself, and the trip from Roanoke to Camp Lejeune was six.

When I could wait no longer, I hugged my mother good-bye and trudged down the steps and the ice-packed driveway to the car. I had deflated my tires, a tip from one of the recruiters, for extra traction on the steep hill and hairpin curve I was facing a few hundred yards from our driveway. News reports on the television that morning were that the highways were fairly clear, but first, I had to scale the hill in front of our home.

My mother was standing on the front porch. She watched me back down the driveway. When I pointed the car into the road and the hill ahead, I noticed she was waving. I rolled down my window and waved above the roof of the car. I let off the brake, gave the car gas, and fishtailed. My mother stopped waving. I tried again. Determined, I released my foot from the brake and let the car ease forward without gas. The closer I got to the bottom of the hill the more pressure I applied to the gas pedal, and then up I went, up the hill, slipping and sliding and fishtailing through the hairpin curve. I wanted to look over my right shoulder to see my mother on the front porch, probably with her hand over her mouth, but I didn't dare. I cleared the curve and rounded the top of the hill. At the top, I blew the horn. I was finally on my own.

I had little difficulty in finding Camp Lejeune. I followed a winding Highway 220 south from Roanoke through Greensboro, and then there had been 70 east through Durham, Raleigh, and Goldsboro. In Kinston, I veered right onto Highway 258 south—the same Highway 258 where ten years later I would contemplate my desertion—and I arrived in Jacksonville around ten that night. I pulled into the parking lot of a gas station to fill the tank once more, and in the head, I changed from civilian clothing to my winter alphas, the formal uniform with jacket, long-sleeved shirtwaist, neck tab, and skirt with pumps. I was a bundle of nervous energy. I was on my own, really on my own now, and eager to make my way. For two weeks after boot camp, I had lived at home while working during the day with recruiters. But at night, my mother had still imposed her eleven-thirty curfew. I was free, or at least as free as a Marine could be, to make my own decisions now.

Streetlights flooded the Camp Lejeune main gate. An MP held up a hand. I rolled down the window. "I'm reporting for duty," I forced out.

"You need to register your car first and get a pass." He motioned toward a building in a brightly lit parking lot.

Inside, I produced my registration, license, and proof of insurance. A corporal glanced through the stapled copies of my orders, tore off a set, and then circled on a faded copy of a base map where I should drive to report for sleeping quarters. Within an hour, I was assigned a room in a co-ed barracks where men were strictly prohibited any access on the third floor and where women were strictly forbidden on the first or second, except for the common areas, which included lounges with televisions. I unlocked the door of my new home and stepped inside. Two single bunks had been placed on opposite sides of a room that was slightly larger than my tiny bedroom in our mobile home. On each bunk was a pile of linen that included two flat sheets, a gray-and-white-striped pillow, a pillowcase, and a green wool blanket with a faded *U.S.* imprint. I set about making both bunks in military style with hospital corners and a taut blanket, as I had learned to do in boot camp. For myself, I chose the bunk closer to the window. The other was closer to the toilet. If I were to have a roommate who might come in during the middle of the night, I thought she would appreciate having a bunk ready to climb into as well as appreciate being closer to the head.

Also in the room were two wall lockers. I opened the one closest to my bunk and found drawers in the bottom and a built-in desk above the drawers. Built-ins along the back wall provided room for hang-up clothing.

The bathroom was tiny with enough floor space for a shower, toilet, and sink, but I didn't mind. After communal showering in boot camp, a head shared with a single roommate seemed luxurious.

Camp Lejeune is about 244 square miles of sandy tank trails, live firing ranges, and beaches for practice assaults. But driving onto the base past the manicured entrance by way of the gently curving tree-flanked boulevard, you might think you'd wandered onto a national park. Yet down any side road, a Harrier jet might be setting down on asphalt as part of a training mission, or a platoon of Marines in full combat gear with rifles might suddenly emerge from a grove of scrubby pines. Despite the Cold War, Marines trained for combat.

My new job, I learned, was far less glamorous. I was assigned to Supply School to learn the basics of loading pallets and warehousing with about forty other men and women. During afternoon breaks, each of us had various jobs: mine was to help admin clerks in the company office. I had been filing paperwork when the company commander, a tall blond with Nordic features, stepped from his office and halted the frenetic activity of admin clerks. He asked for a volunteer to make a soda run.

I jumped to attention. "I'll make the run, Sir."

"You'll need help." This statement had come from the warrant officer with the camera-ready close-up looks. He was tall and leggy, the sort of poster-perfect Marine appearance that had landed him years earlier on the elite Silent Drill Team, and White House guard for President Nixon. He was the first warrant officer I had seen since joining the Marines, and he'd entered the admin office a half hour earlier and had headed straight for the CO's office.

"Ready?" he asked. I'm not sure I answered, but I do remember the glance between him and the CO, and the flutter in my stomach over the idea of being alone with an officer for the first time. The highest-ranking Marine I had been alone with was the gruff first sergeant who seemed to enjoy making me nervous whenever he called me into his office to ask personal questions about my hometown and why I really wanted to be a Marine. One day he called me into the office to ask how I could afford the $120 payment on my new red Chevy Monza hatchback. I still have no idea how he knew about the payment. Another time, he personally inspected my room in the barracks, and finding a replica of a sword—a tin, dull-edged souvenir from the high school halftime performances—he threatened to write me up for possession of a deadly weapon. "Are you kidding, Sir?" I said. "That's not a real sword . . . it couldn't slice bread." He shouted about how naïve I was, and that if he ever found the souvenir in my room again, he'd have me court-martialed. With nowhere to hide it, I gave my high school memories a long, last glance, and tossed the sword into the dumpster outside the barracks.

The warrant officer was waiting for me by the door. I grabbed my headgear. In the cantina that day, Tom and I were the only two Marines in the place. The cantina was a small restaurant beside company headquarters where Marines could buy pizzas and burgers as an alternative to chow-hall food. "Let's sit over here," he said after we'd bought the sodas, pointing toward a table near the back. I was worried about getting back, but like a good sheep I followed him.

"You know," he said after we were settled at the table, "if a certain officer and a certain private were to go out on a date, they'd have to be very discreet. Do you think a private *can* be discreet?"

I was nineteen, and this was 1978. The year we were introduced to the Susan B. Anthony dollar and to the first test-tube baby. The year of the Jim Jones massacre and the return of the Panama Canal to the Panamanians.

I had been a Marine less than four months, and at the bottom of the food chain. An officer had just propositioned me. *This* was called fraternization, and *this* could end your military career. I couldn't imagine why anyone of his stature would take such a risk.

After all, what I'd found most attractive about being a Marine in those early months were the clearly defined boundaries. Rules, I wanted to consume. To stay sober, I had immersed myself in regimentation: reveille at five thirty, in formation by seven, on the job a half hour later, chow three times a day in the mess hall, taps at sunset. Making new friends didn't interest me; new friends would suggest filling up my free hours in the evenings. From my room, where I often kept the door open for fresh air, I heard the others gathering in the common areas around the barracks, orchestrating rides to the enlisted club on base or to the disco clubs in town.

I had also joined the Marines with the understanding that I was subordinating individuality to a collective ideal. In the Marines, I'd envisioned a good hiding place where everyone talked and dressed alike. I couldn't have been more wrong. I was wrong to think the Marines wouldn't praise individual achievement. In boot camp, drill instructors had dangled a set of dress blues and a private-first-class (Pfc.) stripe as incentive for graduating at the top of the platoon. Five pounds of body fat I couldn't shed before the end of boot camp kept me from graduating first, or so the DIs told me.

Despite my initial motives to hide out in the Marines until I could get my life straightened out, there were forces I hadn't suspected working against me. This warrant officer, Tom, who a year later would become my husband, was a crushing force. By putting his career on the line, he was plucking me from obscurity. How intoxicating for a girl whose father had chosen alcohol over . . . let's just say it, *her*.

Tom's question, *Could a private be discreet?* was lingering in the air with the leftover smell of grease from French fries. "I guess that would depend on the private, Sir." I hadn't intended for this to sound coy, but I secretly relished its effect.

Tom lifted his soda, sucked long on the straw.

Tom, who in eighteen months would help me bury my father and become my husband and the father of my only child, walked me back to headquarters. He'd gently, respectfully, taken my arm and guided me toward his left, where an enlisted Marine is supposed to be when walking beside an officer. The Marines we passed along the way gave him snappy salutes, and he said to each, "Good afternoon, Marine," as if it belonged to the refrain of a musical round. It was a cold, gray February afternoon, and I was shivering by the time we reached headquarters. Protocol called for me to open the door for him, and we danced around each other until his hand found the door handle first.

We opened a door to our future that day. Over the next few weeks and several afternoon soda runs, he shared the story of his life. As my father would say, "He was selling himself."

Before his selection to warrant officer, Tom had been a staff sergeant and a DI in San Diego. I learned about his days on the Silent Drill Team, about how he used to trace outlines of trees, buildings, anything with his nose while at the position of attention outside the White House to keep from falling asleep. His year in Vietnam with Third Recon was swiftly mentioned with no room for questions, but he reveled in telling stories from his idyllic childhood. He'd grown up in a small town outside St. Louis, second among six siblings. He had followed his older brother's path into the Marines. Now, this boy from the Show-Me State was flirting with danger. Flirting with a Marine private could get you dishonorably discharged.

A few weeks after the cantina conversation, in preparation for the Inspector General inspection, our CO had designated Tom as our company's representative for inspection in the dress blue uniform. On the morning of the inspection, the CO called me into his office. He was standing beside Tom, who smiled when I entered. He was standing before me, impressive in dress blues with a chest full of medals.

The CO pushed a roll of masking tape into my hand. "Here, tape him off."

"Sir?" I asked, feeling feverish under the sweeping heat of embarrassment. But the CO was already walking out and closing the door behind him.

I was supposed to be the human lint brush. I was supposed to tape away lint from Tom's dress blues before his inspection. The CO's order to make physical contact with another officer was my first exposure to sexual harassment, though I couldn't have fully formed that idea then. Even though I hadn't heard of sexual harassment at nineteen in 1978, I still knew that this order was inappropriate.

Neither of us spoke; it wasn't my place as a private to speak first, and so I proceeded with my task. I tore a long strip of tape and wrapped it around four fingers. I pressed and rolled my hand across his chest and down and between the brass buttons on the front flap of his coat. I taped around his medals, and when they clinked against one another, I whispered, "I'm sorry, Sir." I taped away the lint from the tops of his shoulders and under the epaulets, and when I looked up at him, he was looking down, smiling, as if we shared a secret.

I tore off another long strip from the roll and wrapped it around my fingers. I dragged my sticky hand across his shoulder blades and pressed them into the standing collar around his neck, and then I pressed them downward and downward, following the sharp slope of his back.

For many nights afterward in my room at the barracks, I threw myself on the bunk and closed my eyes to feel the warmth and shape of his body as it had felt under my hand that day.

In the weeks that followed, I saw little of Tom unless he stopped by the CO's office while I was typing up orders or filing during the afternoons immediately following classes from Supply School. A week or so after the IG inspection, I was meritoriously promoted to Pfc. for my recruiting efforts in Roanoke during leave after boot camp. My name had been called out by the CO in front of the three platoons of Headquarters Company during our weekly formation.

Afterward, on my way to Supply School, where I was to take the final exam for warehousing that morning, my path crossed Tom's. He returned my salute, looking down at my collar and flashing a grin when he saw I had wasted no time in pinning on the new rank insignia.

Two weeks later, I was once again called to the front of the formation for another meritorious promotion, this time to lance corporal. I had graduated first in Supply School. After the formation, as others stepped forward to congratulate me, Tom appeared as if he were hanging back on purpose, allowing one Marine after another to move ahead of him in the line. But by the time the last Marine shook my hand, Tom had disappeared. Disappointed, I began the climb up the stairs to my room on the third floor so that I could retrieve my new rank insignia. And there he was, standing on the landing between the second and third floors, waiting. He asked me to dinner.

If I had thought the Marines to be the perfect hideout for me, I had underestimated my insatiable drive for validation, or would it be more accurate to call it approval? Regardless, I had been relentlessly determined to graduate first in Supply School after instructors informed us that a meritorious promotion, which is an accelerated promotion ahead of one's peers, was possible for the top finisher, as well as a career change into a new field since the Supply field was overcrowded. I'm not sure what sort of daily life I had envisioned for myself as a Marine, but I was certain it hadn't included being closed off in a warehouse and on a forklift all day. My worst subject in high school was math, but I willed myself to practice cubic-feet computations and other complicated mathematical puzzles halfway through most nights until I could answer any set of problems correctly. I'm not sure which I wanted more, the promotion or the career change, or simply the validation of accomplishment, something I hadn't felt much of since my family's disintegration. So on a rainy March morning one day after the promotion ceremony to lance corporal, I headed with renewed purpose to the career planner's office at battalion headquarters.

The door to the career planner's office was open. I rapped on the door. The career planner, a staff sergeant, looked up from behind a desk overwhelmed with bulging folders. He pointed to the chair in front of his desk. I gave him my name.

"I don't have you on my re-up list."

"No, Sir, I've only been a Marine for five months. I just finished first in Supply School, and they said whoever finishes first can request a change of MOS. I don't want to be in Supply."

He shrugged and wheeled his chair to a three-shelf bookcase. On each shelf was a row of thick green notebooks. He removed one and wheeled himself back to the desk. While he searched, I scanned his office. To the left of his desk stood a coat tree, from which his headgear and a raincoat were hanging. On his office walls, he had taped reenlistment posters that showed smiling Marines in Far East settings and in European embassy posts, and of Marines dining together in an oceanfront restaurant. Each poster displayed the same message: *Stay Marine!*

"Here." He handed the heavy notebook to me and I scanned the list. There were various aviation maintenance jobs, and jobs in admin, jobs in the chow hall as a cook or baker, jobs in financial disbursing, and so on down the list until I stopped at one that sounded intriguing: military journalist.

"Are you any good at English?"

I smiled. "English was my best subject in high school."

"I'll call Public Affairs to arrange for a test."

Public Affairs was located in a small, white, one-story building on the main road that leads onto Camp Lejeune. On the day of the test, I reported to Master Gunnery Sergeant Phil Harvey. Top Harvey was a short, bald man and, as I would find out later, within a year of retirement. He led me to a desk in a large room where busy reporters were banging on manual typewriters. Several others were huddled in a semicircle, taking turns with a glass that they brought up to their eyes for better looks at a contact sheet of photograph possibilities.

The test had been harder than I imagined. Answering the grammar and punctuation sections was easy, but writing in composition style is much different than writing journalistically. I was clueless on questions that required me to organize information into a lead for a news release, so I improvised with flourish and vocabulary. When finished, I stood before Harvey's desk. He took the test and said to wait in the pressroom.

A few minutes later, a red-faced Harvey stepped inside the pressroom, rapping a yardstick like a metronome against his short legs. He called my name, and I followed him back to his desk. He pointed to the chair beside it. "Look," he said in a tone oddly like my high school guidance counselor's, "you're not a writer. You'll never be a writer."

I was dumbfounded. "Are you sure, Top? I used to get good grades in English composition."

"This isn't English comp. This is journalism."

"But I can learn anything. I just learned how to compute a warehouse of . . ." Just then, a tall, thin man with shocking white hair emerged from an office behind Harvey's desk. Later, I'd learn he was Maj. John Woggon, a.k.a. the Silver Fox, nicknamed so for his white hair and for his eyes, the color of a cold, blue flame.

"Top," he said, "test her on the radio."

"Yes, Sir," Top answered, but the minute we were alone on the broadcast side of the building, he did little to hide his irritation, shoving the radio script, earphones, and microphone at me. I believe he honestly thought he'd weeded out an undesirable.

I had never thought of myself as a radio broadcaster; I had wanted to write copy, not read it. The script was a tongue twister, too. Something about people carrying bags of pennies, a repetitive mess with lots of *p*'s, *r*'s, *s*'s, and *w*'s. After two takes, Top Harvey explained the tape would be mailed to the Defense Information School in Indianapolis for evaluation. Results wouldn't be returned for several weeks.

A few weeks later, the career planner delivered the exciting news that Headquarters Marine Corps had granted my MOS change from Supply to Public Affairs.

When I reported to Public Affairs with my new orders, Top Harvey let me stand this time in front of his desk while he flipped roughly through the paperwork, his thumb wrinkling the bottom right corner of each page. The flipping suddenly halted. His eyebrows lifted, and then narrowed into a single, crooked line. He pushed his chair from the desk, jumped to his feet, and flung the orders to the corner of his desk. Papers scattered to the floor, and I stretched my arms out wildly to catch them as if I thought my life as a journalist depended on them not reaching the floor.

"There's been a mistake," he said. "You were supposed to be approved as a broadcaster, not as a journalist. These orders are all wrong."

I bent to the floor and scrunched under his desk to gather the papers that had escaped me. The career planner that morning hadn't said anything other than I had been approved for a new job in Public Affairs. I had assumed, as Top had apparently, that my new job would be in radio. After all, the write-up evaluation from Indiana about my voice even included a compliment about the solid quality of my voice, except for my *w*'s, which because of my southern upbringing I was pronouncing *dub-yas*.

Harvey was still bemoaning, "How will I *ever* train you to be a writer?"

From under his desk, I implored, "Can't we just ask headquarters to correct the orders?"

"Obviously, you don't know anything about Headquarters Marine Corps . . . we'll never get this fixed."

For several days, Harvey ignored me. He barked out story assignments to others during editorial meetings, assigning a change of command ceremony, an intramural basketball tournament, a fund drive for Navy Relief, and a training exercise involving the amphibious assault of Onslow Beach.

At one of these meetings, the Silver Fox slinked into the pressroom. I heard him direct Top to give me a roll of film and a camera. Top nodded and a few minutes later, called me to his desk. He showed me how to load a 35-millimeter camera and then told me to shoot photos of the major's motorcycle. I would have preferred the large oak tree out back, but I did as I was told.

I snapped photos of the motorcycle, shooting from various angles, bending down to shoot upward. I shot verticals and horizontals, even close-ups on the gauges. When I finished, I handed the camera back to Top Harvey. He took it to the in-house photo techs for development into a contact sheet, and I went back to my desk to wait.

A half hour later, Harvey was walking toward my desk. In one hand, he bounced the yardstick off the side of his leg; in the other, he held the contact sheet. The latter, he pitched on my desk.

"Not bad. Not bad at all."

As a result, he assigned me to cover the next day's change of command ceremony as partner to one of the office's most experienced photojournalists, a sergeant.

The next day, I followed the sergeant from our office to the parade field for the change of command ceremony. On the short walk there, the sergeant filled me in on the details of what I would see: the marching band and the two commanders, the outgoing one and his replacement. Both commanders would step forward as the change of command orders blasted over the loudspeaker, and then the outgoing commander would take the battalion colors—the flag with its battle streamers—and present it to the incoming commander. And then I could expect a parade of marching Marines to pass the reviewing stand, and given the command *Eyes Right!* each platoon would simultaneously snap heads in a single direction toward their new commander until they passed him. Then the platoon would be ordered an *Eyes Front!* It all sounded so important, this recording of history.

At the parade field, military music blasted the air. Official guests and their families were filing into bleachers. Warm ocean breezes from the Atlantic that May afternoon swept through and under dresses, and women fought to hold in place their dignity and their wide-brimmed hats.

The sergeant had disappeared, and so I began taking photos of the band and of the platoons of Marines as they marched in front of the reviewing stand. When the departing colonel turned and handed off the battalion colors to his replacement, I was there, clicking away. When the new battalion commander stepped to the microphone to deliver his message, I was there. When marching Marines passed their commander with an *Eyes Right!* command, I was there. Click, click, click. Nothing, not even the nose hairs peeking from the new commander's left nostril, escaped photographing.

A red-faced Harvey was waiting for me at the side door, his face twisting into ugliness the closer I got. "The major just got a call demanding an official apology for the intrusive disturbance our *woman* Marine caused during the change of command ceremony."

The major appeared at the back door. He refused to look at me. "Top, develop the film and bring the photos to me." He half turned and mumbled, "And they had better be good."

An hour or so later, Major Woggon and Top Harvey emerged from the major's office. Top's face bore what I read as resigned neutrality. The major was beaming at me. "These are the best change of command photographs I've seen." I found out later from Top that the major had called the battalion commander and appeased him with a promise of placement on the front page of the base newspaper.

The day after the change of command ceremony, I walked into the pressroom and found Top Harvey taping to my desk the words: *Who, What, Where, When, How,* and *Why.* Below these he taped: *Time, Date,* and *Place.* He handed me the *Associated Press Style Guide.* "Memorize this." And so, with that, I was on my way toward becoming a military journalist.

Soon afterward, Top began to include me in the upcoming editorial meetings as well. Each of my writing attempts, however, he returned for second, third, and fourth drafts, each bleeding in red ink a little less than the previous one. On the fifth draft, he would often give up and rewrite it himself. The turning point came the day a company commander requested a write-up about one of his lance corporals whose off-duty hobby involved making miniature weapons that actually fired. Top liked the sound of the human-interest angle and assigned it to me.

The Marine had grown up near New York City. I asked him lots of personal questions about why he had joined the Marines, about his family, his job, his goals, and his love for creating miniature weapons. I photographed close-ups of him with his tiny weapons, and then raced back to my desk to prepare the first draft. This time when Top returned the copy, he was beaming. I looked at the single red correction on the first page and flipped to the second page and the third. There were no other corrections. I looked up at Top. "I finally got it right?" Top smiled and walked away, tapping the yardstick against the side of his right leg.

A few months later, Top suddenly smacked the corner of my desk with his yardstick. I jumped. "That story about the New York Marine just got picked up by the *New York Times*. You finally did it . . . you finally proved you're more than a good-looking pair of legs, after all." Despite the personal challenges I had overcome—alcoholism, self-loathing, laziness—I could never defeat the signals my body sent the world. No matter how tight the girdle, I couldn't prevent the swaying of my hips. No matter how small the bra, I couldn't flatten my breasts enough to hide the curves. Uniform regulations insisting on form-fitted shirtwaists created the illusion of an hourglass figure, even on women with stick straight boyish shapes. In the 1980s, the Marine Corps on the whole was fighting the public's stereotype that *nice* girls wouldn't join the Marines.

Oddly, twenty-some years later when I finally attempted to find the *New York Times* story through a number of online searches, I couldn't. In those days before the Internet, we had to rely on word from Headquarters Marine Corps about the civilian newspapers that picked up our stories from the Associated Press, and so it's possible my little story about the Marine who made miniature weapons actually appeared in a different New York newspaper, though I haven't yet discovered which. I have since found the article published in *Leatherneck* magazine.

Besides gathering the news, I found myself often *in* the news. Throughout most of the eighties, reporters were hungry for stories about women in nontraditional jobs, and they frequently requested interviews with women Marines. Later, after becoming a mother, I was often ordered to meet with reporters. Most of the reporters were women. Their first question was always, *Why would a nice girl like you join the Marines?* Nice, by their definition I suppose, was not a woman with obvious femininity who chose to combine the traditional aspects of female life—marriage and motherhood—with the nontraditional military roles usually thought of as male.

One hot, humid Carolina afternoon I was wearing running shorts and a T-shirt and leaning against a wall in a runner's stretch, preparing for the office's mandatory three-mile run, per orders from the Silver Fox. My palms were pressed against the outside wall of our office building, and in a hamstring stretch, when I felt a jab in my upper leg just below my left buttock. I jumped out of the stretch. Major Woggon, the Silver Fox, was standing behind me. With a finger, he again poked into the outer fleshiness of my leg to a lump of forming cellulite. "What is that?"

"Sir?"

He pointed with stronger emphasis to the back of my leg just below the cheek. "What *is* that?"

I looked down at my nineteen-year-old thighs that ran a minimum of fifteen miles a week, and saw them for the first time as somehow disconnected from my body. When I looked up, the Silver Fox was gone, jogging up ahead on the sidewalk. That night, in front of my bathroom vanity mirror, I examined my backside. I held up a hand mirror to check out the rear view. My legs were lean and muscular, hard even, except for a plushy feel of embryonic fat on the upper outer area of each leg. The Silver Fox's public pinpointing of a flaw had dredged up the old insecurities about how I was less than normal, even less what a man might find desirable, and, looking back, this would become another defining moment that would drive me throughout my twenties to prove otherwise, jeopardizing both my marriage and my career.

Tom and I married two months after my father's death, six months after Major Woggon's humiliating finger-jabbing episode. When the major discovered I had married an officer, he called me to his office and lectured me about fraternization, threatening to charge us both with fraternization under the Uniform Code of Military Justice. My knees were trembling as I stood in front of his desk. I could still feel the imprint of shame from his finger poke on my leg. What he didn't know as he stood there blustering with threats was that my husband had allies at Headquarters Marine Corps in DC, and orders were on the way that would reassign us to Okinawa.

★

On November 4, 1979, the day Iranian militants stormed the
American Embassy in Tehran and began a 444-day standoff with
about seventy hostages, I was standing outside the Naha airport
terminal in Okinawa, Japan, longing for sunglasses. Back then,
in my twenties, I refused to wear them, believing that once you
let yourself get used to something, you could become a slave to it
forever. The Marine lieutenant carrying my suitcase to the sedan
confirmed this. "Wait a minute," he said, dropping the suitcase
on the sidewalk and digging into a pocket for a pair of aviators.
"The sun's brighter here than in the States."

Tom found his sunglasses, too, put them on, and motioned
for me to catch up. I shifted my carry-on bag to the opposite
shoulder and looked up, shielding my eyes with a free hand.
Above us, laundry hanging from every floor of concrete apartment
complexes shimmied in the tropical November breeze. "C'mon,
Marine!" my husband teased. We'd been married six months by
then—technically still newlyweds.

My feet, swollen from the nineteen-hour flight, were spilling
out of my high heels; each step felt as though I were walking on
the tops of my ankles. At least my feet were managing to move
forward. My mind was still refusing to budge across the International Dateline. I hadn't wanted these orders to Okinawa. A
month earlier, I had been four months pregnant in Jacksonville,
North Carolina, planning our baby's nursery. One evening, Tom
had come home crestfallen by the news that he was being shipped
overseas for a year. We knew military orders separated couples

all the time, but for some reason, we had expected our first year of marriage to grant us immunity from such things as military separations and miscarriages.

Naha is the busy capital city of Okinawa Prefecture on Okinawa Island. Taxi drivers were blaring horns. Okinawan children in navy-and-white school uniforms circled magazine stands and bus stops. An old woman with bright eyes and no teeth, wearing a knee-length gray tunic and slip-on shoes, smiled at me as she walked by, swinging a full plastic grocery bag that balanced her bowlegged sway. I was surrounded by a dizzying sea of colorful billboards marked with strange symbols and Asian faces. Most advertisements were impossible to make out. Others were easier: a Coca-Cola billboard across the street; the face of a young Asian woman, delicate, lotus-like, smiling beside the Nikon camera she held in her palm.

I was twenty that first day in Okinawa. Stateside, before the miscarriage, I'd felt as if I were finally coming into my own, despite the lack of control I had over my life as a Marine. But such is the life of a Marine: a life lived on the altar of sacrifice. I may have survived boot camp at Parris Island and certainly my share of sexual harassment from senior officers, but a few minutes in a foreign country with its unreadable billboards and its left-side driving were fast producing the sense that I was unraveling and disconnecting from my body.

I hobbled the rest of the sidewalk outside of the Naha airport to the sedan and to Tom, who was flashing a wide smile. He laid my carry-on bag across our suitcases and squeezed my hand. "Everything's going to be fine." I forced a smile through the fear that I might float away like a released balloon over the South China Sea if he were to let go of my hand.

From the back seat of the sedan, Tom looked odd in the left-front passenger seat without a steering column in front of him. An empty space that seemed in need of filling. I ran my hand across my belly, across an empty womb that shouldn't have been.

Our Marine lieutenant friend slid into the right-front side behind the steering wheel. "You can't go more than twenty-one miles-per-hour on the whole goddam island." He searched over his shoulder for a break in the oncoming traffic. "But, it won't be the hardest thing about Okinawa you'll have to get used to. This place is full of surprises." He floored the gas, and we lunged into a lane that opened when a taxi stopped for a fare. I watched his ease in shifting gears, left hand in sync with left foot, and I practiced in the back seat, shifting imaginary gears with an imaginary clutch until the left side of my body felt oddly overused.

"Genghis Khan," he said, "that restaurant there." He was pointing toward a small concrete building on the right with glass windows. Between the panes of glass, a waterfall. "They have the best Mongolian barbecue on the island."

Tom swiveled to face me. "Hear that? Mongolian barbecue!" He loved this. It was his first time to Okinawa, but eight years older than I, this man my father had warned wasn't mature enough for me had been with Third Recon during Vietnam in 1968. Before heading to Vietnam, he had taken scuba training in the Philippines. To Tom, this was merely another adventure. Adventure to me meant risk-taking. Taking a risk meant losing an element of self-control, and losing self-control could lead to all sorts of bad behavior patterns I preferred to think I'd left somewhere on the other side of the International Dateline.

Near the crest of a hill, our friend had said, "You won't want to miss this view." I leaned toward the center of the back seat and saw the Pacific Ocean and a few distant islands that make up the Ryukyu Island chain opening before us. What did I know about this tiny island that was to become our home for a year? I knew it was sixty-seven miles long and between two to fourteen miles wide. I knew Okinawa was often described as a tropical paradise with a lush landscape that crept down mountain canyons to the shoreline. Commodore Perry, after anchoring in the Naha port in 1853, had struggled for words: "It would be difficult for you to imagine the beauties of this island with respect to the charming scenery and the marvelous perfection of cultivation." And I knew that the battle for Okinawa in 1945 had been one of the bloodiest of the war. More than fifty thousand Marines and soldiers were killed, unable to defend themselves against wave after wave of kamikaze pilots. A hundred and twenty thousand Japanese had died. Particularly heart wrenching to me were the stories about Okinawan women who, during the bloody battle, had climbed to the tops of these cliffs and tossed their babies to the sea. Some mothers leapt after their babies; others had held tightly to their little ones and stepped into airy nothingness. Those too afraid to take the leap had been shoved over the cliffs by fathers, brothers, and uncles. Death was preferred to the dishonor of capture, and from what they believed would be rape and torture by U.S. Marines.

I peered out the car window at the jutting rocks below and felt my stomach curl inside out. I couldn't imagine tossing my baby to the sea. On this particular day, the South China Sea was placid, inviting. Coral beds, white sand, and painfully clear skies created jewel-toned water that graduated from the palest green near the shore to the dark blue of a newborn's eyes out on the horizon.

Two months after our wedding a Navy doctor informed me I had probably conceived on the honeymoon. This had been his estimation after studying the paperwork in my chart and counting backward from my last menstrual cycle.

"But we hadn't planned on having a baby right away," I said, giving way to the nurse's soft touch to my shoulder in an attempt to have me lie back on the examination table.

The doctor had disappeared into that space under the paper sheathing. I heard him say from down there, "These things have a way of planning themselves."

"But my husband has orders to Okinawa in a few months . . . you know headquarters won't send a pregnant Marine to Okinawa." On the ceiling was a poster of palm trees and ocean, an image I'd thought particularly cruel, given that my husband was headed to the tropics for a year without me. Up until 1977, the year I'd joined the Marines, pregnant military women were forced out of the service. But now, pregnant women could choose to leave the service or stay. I could appreciate the right to choose even if I did not care for either choice.

The doctor snapped off the latex gloves and tossed them into a wastebasket by the door. "You won't be the first Marine or the first military wife to have a baby alone."

And months later, after the miscarriage, after recovering from the procedure that had sucked away the last proof of baby and placenta (with Tom folded in the chair beside the hospital bed, asleep, possibly dreaming about the two children he already had with his ex-wife . . .), I would recall my doctor's claim that these things have a way of planning themselves, not knowing then— but how could anyone?—that I was to conceive during our first night in the village of Ginoza on Okinawa.

"Notice how all the cars are white here?" our tour guide friend was saying as he drove northward from the Naha airport to the base at Henoko. I could see his eyes in the rearview mirror, and so I nodded, although truthfully, I hadn't noticed white cars at all.

When he downshifted into a sharp curve, the car sputtered. "It's so hot here," he said, "that nobody but the Japanese mafia drives black cars." Then he winked into the rearview mirror. "Don't worry. You'll know the Yakuza by their black cars and by their missing pinkies." My eyebrows must have lifted into a question. "Here," he said, and held up his left hand, thumb pressed against the final joint of his little finger. "To show loyalty to each other."

While Tom and the lieutenant shared stories about the Marines they had lost touch with through the years, I held firmly to the armrest of the car door with my right hand and with the left, balanced my weight against the back seat as we whipped around curves, passing fields and fields of tall sugar cane, the sudden spring-up of villages, and the mama-sans who were toting groceries in their arms and babies on their backs. I thought again about the baby we had lost, the loss we had both mourned: yet hadn't I detected Tom's relief? He had two children, and had never been keen on the idea of having more. At times, I could believe he even resented me for the pregnancy, for the baby had been the reason we were facing a year's separation.

The Yakuza severed pinkies to prove loyalty.

My body had given up a child.

The first two weeks on Okinawa, we lived in the BOQ, bachelor officers' quarters, at the island's most northern base, Camp Henoko. An enlisted Marine who was married to an officer and living in the BOQ was breaking all regulations of military fraternization. Tom's CO had made it clear the arrangement was a temporary fix until we could find housing off base.

So each morning, I dressed in cammies and combat boots and walked to the front gate, where I would wait for one of the military buses that made the rounds from base to base. I was a military journalist, assigned to cover combat training at Camp Hansen, a base located a forty-minute bus ride from Henoko.

On the way to the bus stop each morning, I would pass a flurry of mama-sans who were coming on base to clean each Marine's quarters and to wash and press clothing and shine boots. And each evening, as I stepped off the bus and walked up the hill that provided a jaw-dropping view of the South China Sea, I would pass the mama-sans on their way home.

Every morning they waved and giggled. Every evening the same. I couldn't imagine what opinion they had of me. I was the only woman Marine on the base. I wondered what role they imagined I played in the company, and service, of these men.

At the end of our first two weeks, Mr. Tamiyaki, the head guard of the base ammunition depot, informed us of an apartment that had become available in the nearby village of Ginoza. The apartment had been leased by his friend Kyoko, who had moved out the day before. Mr. Tamiyaki drove us into the village to see the apartment. We followed him up the concrete steps to the second floor.

"Only one left in whole village," he said as he turned the doorknob and elaborately swept his left hand as a signal for us to enter. He remained outside, smoking his rolled cigarette and hovering by the doorframe. A shrewd move given the limitation of space in the tiny apartment.

What can I say? The apartment was bleak. Two rooms and a bath. A Formica kitchen table, four chairs. A straw futon bed in the bedroom. I joined Tom on the edges of the lumpy bed. From around the corner, Mr. Tamiyaki called out, "Nice bed!" I choked on a giggle.

Tom whispered. "At least we'll have a Western toilet."

"With directions, too." Someone had taped onto the back of the toilet tank a label that depicted stick figures in both the sitting and standing positions.

We fell across the bed laughing toward the ceiling, the kind of laughter that refused to be corralled, the kind of laughter we hadn't shared since losing the baby. The mattress was stiff, prickly. I rolled over to look at Tom; the corners of his eyes were moist.

"Look," I said, beating on a hard lump of straw, "only one left in whole village."

At nine that first night in Ginoza, between the bars on the windows of our new apartment, I could see the village lights. The pungent odor of cooked fish, ginger, and soy floated in with the night air. Two military men in T-shirts and jeans, carrying bottles of beer, stumbled through the doorway of a bar, spilling disco music into the street.

A tiny Asian woman with long black hair was chasing after them in her short skirt and high heels. "GIs, you wait for me!" She wedged her body between them and guided the threesome into a dark alley. Laughter. A sound like the crashing of glass on pavement, most likely an empty beer bottle thrown toward one of Ginoza's open sewers.

Somewhere out there in the village, Tom was walking shore patrol. It was a military payday, and red taxis were ferrying Marines and sailors to and from Camps Henoko and Schwab on the one road that led into and out of Ginoza: one road that looped past our apartment and then along the edge of the Pacific, passing bars, teahouses, seamstress shops, an appliance store with refrigerators left outside to weather the elements, and past ornate wooden homes with Shinto lion heads to guard against demons.

Behind me in the tiny kitchen were the suitcases that needed unpacking, and ahead of me the chore of transforming the two rooms into something romantic, even if Tom wouldn't be home until after midnight, even if I hadn't wanted him in the same way for several weeks now, since the miscarriage. I'd blamed the loss of our baby on the stress of facing childbirth alone and a year without my husband. And secretly, I had blamed Tom, although when I was honest with myself, I could admit he had no more control over his life as a Marine than I.

I pulled myself from the window view of Ginoza to store the milk, orange juice, and several containers of yogurt in the miniature refrigerator, and discovered I hadn't room for the apples. Arranged in a cereal bowl on the table, they gave the room a homey look, I thought.

I covered the straw mattress with borrowed linens from the officers' quarters. Two plates, two cereal bowls, four spoons, four forks, four knives, and four glasses, all borrowed as well, I placed in a single cabinet above the sink. There was no stove, only a single gas burner. But then, we had no pots.

Around midnight, I finished unpacking and stepped back to imagine the apartment as Tom would see it in a few hours. Food in the refrigerator. The apples in a bowl on the table. In the bathroom, a cake of soap, fresh towels and washcloths stacked on a shelf. In the bedroom, I had arranged our civilian clothes, uniforms, and shoes in the built-in wardrobe. I set our alarm clock on the floor by the bed and collapsed onto the lumpy straw mattress.

Around one thirty, someone banged on the apartment's metal door, and I jumped from the bed. I heard, "Kyoko!" in a non-English accent. On the way to the door, I tripped over the empty suitcases beside the kitchen table, knocking the bowl of apples to the floor when my hand reached for something to break my fall, and now several deep voices were shouting, "Kyoko!" and hammering on the door.

I called out, "Kyoko . . . not here. *Gome nasia.* I'm sorry." The banging and shouting continued. Had they mistaken me for Kyoko? I heard breaking glass. Laughter. They kicked at the door. "Kyoko!"

I could have flung open the door, stunned them with my

American presence, flashed an arrogant how-dare-you-look . . . but I couldn't imagine that this was the safest option. I glanced toward the windows and between the bars at the village where Tom was walking shore patrol. The kicking and shouting continued. I waited for a lull, and when their shouts subsided, I answered, "Kyoko not here. No Kyoko. You. Go. *Away!*" There had been a final kick, a little mumbling, and then footsteps. The footsteps gradually fell softer as they descended the staircase and disappeared into the reverberating hum of Ginoza.

As I collected the spilled apples from the kitchen floor, I wondered about this woman they called Kyoko. If they had known her intimately enough to think she would have expected them at this hour, how had they not known she had moved? A flash entered my mind of the Asian woman I'd seen herding the two military men into the dark alley beside the bar. Was Kyoko a prostitute? Is this why so many had come calling so late?

I stood beside the straw bed. Earlier I had lain there thinking that this bed, with all its lumps and bumps, was about to become the centerpiece of my new life with Tom in this foreign country. Now all I could imagine as I stared at the bed was that it must have been the centerpiece to Kyoko's life as a prostitute. I had covered her bed with our linens. Filled her refrigerator with our food. Our clothes were hanging in her wardrobe. Would we have taken the apartment had we known? "Only one left in whole village." And how many voices had I heard on the other side of the door? Three? Four? I pictured them all looking a little like Mr. Tamiyaki, rolling their cigarettes on the Formica table, helping themselves to Orion beer from the tiny refrigerator, waiting their turn.

It was after 3:00 a.m. before Ginoza fell asleep. The squeal of taxis braking for the sharp curve in front of our building and the intermittent disco music that had earlier been regulating my heartbeat had finally ceased. I hadn't found sleep possible.

In Kyoko's bed, I lay naked, spread-eagled, staring at the ceiling Kyoko must have stared at as she lay beneath each man. Had she counted the shadows cast by the bars in the windows? Had there been no other choice for her than this life? Was this choice a deliberate one, although born of sad circumstances? In my mind played the scene of men and their escalating voices at the kitchen table, waiting for Kyoko to satisfy first one and then another before she sent them all back out into the village.

In this proud culture where women had once tossed their babies to the sea and leapt to their deaths to avoid humiliation, women had turned to prostitution. How sad that Kyoko had become a slave to the whims of others. And yet, I'm embarrassed to admit I also felt a strange and erotic admiration sweep over my body as I imagined the kind of power Kyoko must have held over all the men she brought into our bed. As a new wife, I found it frightening to lose this kind of control to someone. Before I was able to will myself into sobriety, I had used alcohol to unleash my inhibitions. I had become a slave to the heady cocktail of alcohol and sex, although I still do not know why. But the young woman I was that night lying in Kyoko's bed—body tingling from the mind's wild fantasies—began to convince herself that she no longer needed alcohol to enjoy sex. That if, instead, she were to develop enough of Kyoko's skill, perhaps she could also develop enough confidence to release herself wholly to her husband.

In the weeks since the miscarriage, I hadn't wanted Tom at all, though there were nights I had pretended and had allowed it to happen. Lying in Kyoko's bed that first night in Ginoza, I realized that it must have been a little like that for her. Surely, she must have had her favorites: a man with beneficent skill and a Hollywood smile. Perhaps she had even become pregnant, and . . . I reached to the floor for the alarm clock. In fifteen minutes, Tom was due to be relieved of shore patrol, home in less than thirty.

Just then, another knock on the door, a whisper of a knock. "Kyoko?" This time the voice was deep, from an American, and this time I did not answer. His knocking turned urgent. "Kyoko . . . are you there, Kyoko?" I pictured him young, a Marine with a bulging wallet of payday cash, dressed in a T-shirt and jeans like the two who had sneaked into the alley with their black-haired girl. Again he whispered imploringly, "Kyoko? Are you there?" A part of me wanted to slip from the bed, tiptoe to the door, and whisper, "Kyoko's gone . . . I live here now." Instead, I wiggled my naked body into the mattress until it felt buoyed among the lumps and bumps of straw, floating toward the sound of my husband's key in the lock.

★

Soon after, I discovered I was pregnant.

Tom and I resolved to keep the pregnancy secret for a while. We knew if Public Affairs discovered I was pregnant, I would be ordered south to Camp Butler, the main base nearly a two-hour drive from Tom's base at Henoko.

During this time, my job was to write articles about Marine life at Camp Hansen, sending them south via driver to the main office at Butler. One day, my boss, a woman gunnery sergeant, assigned me to cover an amphibious operation off the coast of Camp Schwab. My job was to ride along and capture photographs of the school of vehicles as it floated toward the ship and of the first vehicles to enter the belly of the ship, and then move topside to photograph the first vehicles splashing down the ramp to the sea. In those days, we called the vehicles AMTRAKS because on land they run on tracks like a tank; in water, they're a boat without an escape hatch. Marines called them floating coffins.

Tom was frantic when I told him about the assignment. He was pacing the living room of our tiny apartment. "You have to tell them you're pregnant."

"We agreed no one should know yet."

"I can't bear the thought of how something could go wrong and you'd be trapped down there. There's no escape."

I had gone anyway, and the morning of the exercise I met the Marines of Amphibious Assault Platoon on the Camp Schwab beach. The Pacific was whitecapping that day beyond the ring of coral reef. The gray sky and cool breeze cast an ominous message.

I shivered, despite being bundled in a heavy field jacket. A movement on the rocky edge of the cliff above caught my attention and I looked up, finding Tom there with his arms folded across his chest. I waved. He turned and left.

I trudged through the thick sand to report to the platoon commander, a first lieutenant. "Listen, Sergeant," he shouted against the stiff breeze, "the ship's captain is hopping mad that we're bringing a woman aboard. He says he'll have to stay in his cabin until the exercise is over—you know, bad luck for a Navy captain to see a woman on his ship. I don't want to rub salt in this, so I want you to just lay low after you're aboard. Stay out of sight."

The irony of the Navy captain's superstition compared to what I might be truly sacrificing was not lost on me.

Soon after the ship exercise, the secret of my pregnancy was out, and sure enough, my Marine bosses, which included Major Woggon again, reassigned me south. Tom had to make the long drive north every day. We moved into a one-room downtown apartment where roaches the size of baby mice chewed through the cellophane bread wrappers and crawled over us at night.

At one doctor's appointment, a Navy doctor ordered an ultrasound. After I was prepped and waiting for the doctor, Tom had stepped down the hallway to use the restroom. A stern Navy nurse wouldn't allow him back in after the ultrasound had begun.

The doctor passed the wand over my bloated, jellied belly and pronounced, "You're five months along."

"Five? Are you sure only five? I'm huge." Since the miscarriage before our departure to Okinawa, my cycle had been irregular, and Tom and I had decided, because of my size, I was further along.

"Five months. But look . . ." he said, and squished the wand across my belly. "Here's one head . . ." he moved the wand to the other side, "and here's the second head. Twins. But, yep, you're only five months."

After the ultrasound, I found Tom reading a golf magazine in the lobby.

"What's wrong?" he said.

"Can you believe I'm only five months?" I looked down at my enormous belly.

"You're kidding." He returned the magazine to a rack on the wall and helped me by the arm down the single flight of stairs to the first-floor lobby.

"I have another four months to go." I sobbed during the long, muggy walk across the hospital parking lot to the car, wiping sweat from my face with a handkerchief I stopped to pull from my purse. May in Okinawa felt like August back home. We had no air conditioning at our apartment or in our white Toyota. Tom had run ahead to open the door for me. I waddled toward the car, sobbing, imagining how much more miserable I would be at a heavier weight, carrying twins through the sweltering summer months to the end of August, and that's when, for the first time since the ultrasound, I remembered the news about the twins. Struggling to squeeze inside the tiny car, I blurted the news.

For a moment, Tom's face went as blank as the encyclopedia salesman's face had that night in our living room. "You're joking," he said. I struggled to squeeze back out of the car, grabbed his hand, and led him back to the hospital, back up the stairs, and back down the long hallway to the door marked *Ultrasound*.

The doctor grinned when we entered. "Doc, tell him," I said, "tell him we're about to have twins, made in Japan!"

At six months along, the doctors placed me on bed rest and threatened to hospitalize me if my blood pressure didn't lower. We moved closer to Tom's work, to Kin Village, to a three-room apartment above the appliance store run by our mama-san and papa-san, who lived in the apartment at the rear of their store.

It was June, hot, humid, and without air conditioning. I was swelling into dangerous probability of toxic shock.

The doctors ordered weekly appointments, and since I could no longer reach the pedals because I had to push the seat so far back from the steering wheel to accommodate my belly, Tom took off from work each week to drive me south to the hospital at Camp Butler. Those trips were the only freedom I had from the apartment, and I enjoyed the moving picture show of winding roads past sugar cane fields and through villages and store windows with displays of Shinto dogs and replicas of Samurai swords. *Samurai*, to serve. *Ohayo gozaimasu*, good morning. *Konbanwa*, good evening. *Konnichiwa*, good afternoon. *Sayonara*, good-bye. *Arigato*, thank you. These simple phrases were the extent of my Japanese.

Each week, a doctor measured my belly and reminded me that the babies could come any day. "I wish they would hurry," I said during one of the appointments.

"No, you don't," the doctor said. "Every day in here," and he patted my tummy, "is another day for them to grow and be able to survive after birth. We don't want preemies if we can help it, but with twins, it's normal for them to come early."

The twins must have been listening, for they continued growing, and I passed through hot June and miserable July and most of August. I looked like someone who had strapped on a bass drum. Maternity blouses stopped short, leaving the stretchy panel of my maternity pants visible. I could no longer reach my own belly button.

At what would become the final check-up, I pleaded with my doctor to induce labor. For two weeks, my blood pressure had hovered around 200/110, and I had been dilated three centimeters and was experiencing false labor. "They aren't moving as much as they used to," I said. "I'm afraid something will go wrong if we wait much longer."

"Nonsense. All babies slow their movements as they get closer to birth."

Then he chastised me, saying the babies couldn't weigh but a few pounds each, and didn't I want two healthy children? and if I did, and of course so, then I needed to carry them for as long as possible.

Six days later, on their due date and on the forward edge of a typhoon pressing for the island, I went into labor around four thirty in the afternoon. Tom drove me to the hospital, neither of us truly convinced this was it. But the examination revealed I was dilated six centimeters.

At midnight, everything went horribly wrong. Nurses took turns searching for the second baby's heartbeat. "I'll bet," said a nurse who was trying to muster a reassuring tone, "one is just turned, hiding, and that's why we're not hearing the heartbeat."

When I was ready to push, the doctor had me taken to the operating room in the event a Caesarean might be required. A half hour later, Morgan was born, weighing 7.14 pounds, and I remember the sweet mew of her cry and then the sudden shouts from the doctor. "Get him out of here," he said several times, and the nurses ushered my stunned husband from the operating room. A mask went over my face and everything disappeared: the lights; the sounds; Tom, who had been holding my hand; our daughter's cry.

When I came to, a nurse was standing across the room.

"Was it a boy or a girl?"

"The other baby didn't make it."

"Oh."

"Let me get your husband," she said. "He's been awfully worried about you."

Tom was standing by my side as if he'd been there all along, a blink away. His eyes were red.

"Was it a boy or a girl?"

"A girl."

"What happened? How's the other baby? Is she okay?"

"She's fine. The second one was stillborn."

Jennifer, at 7.2 pounds, had become entangled in her umbilical cord when she tried to turn for delivery a week or so earlier, and she had suffocated. My instincts about my babies had been right; the doctors, in thinking the twins weren't more than five pounds each, dead wrong.

Tom and our friends—a married couple whose baby had been born two weeks before ours—later described the scene that occurred when the Navy doctor walked out of the operating room, shaking his head. Tom had misread the gesture, thinking it was I who had died, and he'd lunged for the doctor, throwing him against a wall.

Sometime later, as the weighty loss of a daughter seeped into consciousness, Tom appeared beside the bed, in his arms a bundle of healthy newborn, on his face an expression of something truly fearful, as if he'd just seen a ghost. "You're not going to believe who she looks like," he said.

She had to look like him, I remember thinking. Don't most newborns favor their fathers as nature's offer of genetic truth? I reached for my baby. Tom placed her in my arms, and I gasped. She didn't look like Tom. She didn't look like me. For one day, and one day only, Morgan looked exactly like my father.

It had been impossible to rejoice over Morgan's birth while we were mired with guilt. Hadn't I sensed my babies were ready? Hadn't I pleaded with the doctor? Tom made all the calls to family back in the States. I would eventually write the letters. I didn't want to hear my mother's reassuring voice or anyone else's say, *Things happen for a reason*, or, *Things have a way of working out for the best*. To hell with that. My daughter was dead.

Marines from the Public Affairs office showed up with flowers and grim faces. No one knew how to respond. *Congratulations on your baby, sorry for your loss?* During the somber memorial service at an Okinawan crematorium days later, only Tom, Morgan, and I, by choice, said our prayerful good-byes to Jennifer Gayle. Her remains, in a small black lacquered urn with elaborate gold lettering in Japanese I still haven't translated, have followed me through every move all these years. Tom and I dreaded going back to the apartment, where two of everything awaited us. When Mama-san and Papa-san saw us pull in front of the appliance store and emerge with Morgan in my arms, they rushed from the store, smiling and shouting, *Roun' Eyes, Roun' Eyes!* Mama-san looked from the baby in my arms to my husband. She appeared confused; her eyes lifted into a question mark and she held up a single finger. I nodded and burst into tears.

Shortly afterward, there was the grating sound of sawing on the outer wall of our bedroom. Tom walked out on the balcony to investigate.

"It's Papa-san," he yelled back. "He's cutting a hole in the wall."

"What on earth for?" I said, carrying Morgan to the bedroom for a look. "There's a typhoon on the way."

Papa-san's face materialized in our bedroom, hilariously framed by the new square hole in the wall. Over his shoulder I saw the window air conditioner. Papa-san was grinning. *Too hot . . . too hot fo' baby-san.*

TWO

★

Two months after Morgan was born, Tom and I found ourselves reassigned to Camp Pendleton in southern California. Those early years in the Marines and in my marriage to Tom and as a new mother felt ripe with exciting possibility. No one could have convinced me otherwise. Now, thirty years later, since leaving the Marines under conditions that were less than honorable, I have nothing but time and stories to tell. Stories about the Marines who served with me, about the honor of serving a cause greater than the self, about betrayals—my own and those who betrayed me, although these I hope to tell in the voice of forgiveness for all of us.

Through the years, if you had asked me why I left the Marines, I'm sorry to say I would have lied to you. I would have offered you a litany of excuses. I might have said I left to apply my skills as a military journalist in the civilian world. Or that the divorce had caused me to want a separation from military life altogether. Or that a combination of all these made the timing for a significant life change all the more imperative. And if you were to ask me today, I would probably still lie and save us both the embarrassment the truth would cause us.

Today, I live on the Gulf Coast of Florida. I'm learning to accept that salt water breaks down everything. The window sills. The nails on the dock. Even my resolve to withhold the truth about the old me, or rather the young me.

In the garage, I have compiled a new list of emergency supplies, as I do at the beginning of each hurricane season. I have remarried, as has Tom, and my new husband and I live less than fifty feet from the bay, less than nine above sea level. For a man who once played pro baseball—living out of hotels in a different city nearly every three days—and for a woman who was once a Marine (now a journalism professor at a nearby private college), living on the edge of impending change is all we've ever known.

On this day, I am rummaging through a large rubber container. I have already discarded the year-old batteries and the snack bars and bottled water with March expiration dates, and have jotted these items onto a page of a notebook when I make the mistake of glancing across the garage at my military footlocker. Years earlier, I brokered an agreement with my new husband stipulating that during evacuation mode, my footlocker was to receive the same priority as the rubber container with the canned beans and toilet paper.

Kneeling before this footlocker, I lift the lid and expose its contents to a misty stream of dust motes floating in from the garage windows. I am searching for something and nothing in particular. If I close my eyes, the smell of ink from the stack of newspaper clippings of stories I wrote in the eighties can reel me back into frantic pressrooms of Public Affairs offices where young reporters like me (all of us then around the ages of my college sophomore students) banged on manual typewriters to a background cacophony of arguments between editors and writers. As a sergeant in Public Affairs, later an officer, I saw more of the Corps in those days than the average Marine. No two days for a military journalist were ever alike. You might find yourself flying in a helicopter flown by Secretary of the Navy John Lehman on Monday; orchestrating a press conference for Secretary of the Interior William Clark on Wednesday; and riding with grunts in a tank on Friday.

It was Harry Truman who said the Marines had a propaganda machine nearly as good as Stalin's, and as a military journalist for Public Affairs I played a role in propagating that propaganda. My job for ten years had been to tell the Marine Corps story in ways that were sure to increase our recruitment and retention levels. As one Public Affairs officer made it clear when I tried sneaking in negative sensory details about the effects of heat on Marines engaged in a desert exercise, *Your job is to make Marines feel good about their Corps and the public feel good about its Marines.*

As a military journalist, I had written a variety of stories for release to the public. I wrote about our efforts to preserve a herd of bison that roamed the northern hills of Camp Pendleton and our efforts to protect nesting sea turtles at Onslow Beach at Camp Lejeune, North Carolina. I wrote about the landing craft exercises in the South China Sea in Okinawa. I conducted interviews with living Medal of Honor recipients. I wrote about Marines who were training for the Olympics, and about those who did little else than train for war. I interviewed actor Robert Conrad about his repeated interest in playing Marine roles, and learned he had sneaked into the Marines at fifteen and considers himself as having been a Marine, even if for only thirty-two hours until a girlfriend reported his age to recruiters. These, and many more, were the stories released to the AP and UPI wire services.

A good press release in those days included aspects about daily life for a Marine, about combat exercises, beach assaults, helicopter gunships, and bombing raids with five-hundred-pounders that shook the earth like a quake. Live-fire bombings always produced an angry outpouring from the public, who called our office to complain about lost knickknacks from their bookcases, about broken china and shattered windows and mirrors, about the spidery fissures creeping steadily across their drywall. Some callers needed reassurance America wasn't under Soviet attack. One caller, who after being assured we were conducting live-fire exercises, laughed nervously and said the rumble of a five-hundred-pounder was becoming for him the new sound of freedom. I shared it was unfortunate our previous caller couldn't express the same enthusiasm—she had lost her grandmother's china. "A small price to pay," he'd added.

The eighties had been a relatively quiet era in military history if you discounted Cold War threats, the Noriega arrest, the invasion of Grenada, the peacekeeping mission in Beirut that turned anything but peaceful, and the bombing raid on Gadhafi's Tripoli. Cold war or hot, I guess the only thing more stressful in the eighties than facing combat was the constant training for it. And that's what Marines did, even Public Affairs Marines who practiced how to set up field offices and communication routes for press releases. We escorted news media via helicopter to aircraft carriers that were bobbing out in the Pacific or in the Atlantic so that film crews could get their footage of jet takeoffs and landings. We escorted news media aboard landing craft and fished them out of the surf when they stumbled behind the Marines they were trying to film, the Marines who would have gladly run over them to storm a beach and set up fields of fire against artificially manufactured enemies.

The money from the Defense Department was flowing from Capitol Hill in those days with Casper Weinberger as our secretary of defense. I was writing stories about the new laser-guided weapon systems that could melt the densest Soviet tank armor and new aircraft like the Osprey, which was part plane, part helicopter. President Reagan, for most of the decade, was our commander in chief, followed by the first George Bush, and both men seemed compelled to improve upon the philosophy that a good show of force around the world was the surest, safest way toward staving off an attack.

And so, while our military pumped iron for a fight that in the end was never fought, the Soviets—Reagan's "Evil Empire"—fell, exhausted from the benign effort. For Marine infantry, in particular, those years must have seemed a cycle of relentless, monotonous hovering on the edge of what they simultaneously feared would be their calling and what they feared would be their missed opportunity.

For women Marines, at least for me, every day in the eighties—that decade with the mantra *You-can-have-it-all*—felt fresh with battle, with new hills to take, oppressors to overcome, and internal demons to subdue.

What you wouldn't have read in a Marine Corps press release was anything negative unless a Marine had been injured or killed, and then news releases were dispatched as quickly to the media as we could verify next of kin notification. One night, as a twenty-two-year-old sergeant at Camp Pendleton, I was spending the night as the Public Affairs Marine on duty. I was asleep on a single bunk in the back room when the telephone rang. My watch read two thirty. I jumped to my feet before the end of the second ring and flipped on the light, stumbling back to a desk beside the head of the bunk to answer the telephone and for the notepad and pen I kept handy in the event of phone calls such as this one.

"Public Affairs . . ." I answered, unable to get my name and rank out before the gravelly voice of a Military Police officer blurted out the details of a civilian plane that had crashed into the middle of a tent city where Marines were being housed as part of a combat exercise. Inside your head, you're thinking, *Why my watch?* You know this means you'll have to talk to the media; no one in Public Affairs relished talking with the media for fear of being misquoted or having a statement taken out of context, which happened frequently.

I went to work, asking the Military Police officer on the other end of the phone line the typical questions I knew to ask from the earliest days of my journalism training with Top Harvey: What time did the accident occur? What units were affected? What type of plane? How many aboard? How many in the plane killed? How many on the ground injured or killed?

I jotted onto the notepad his answers: *approximately 12:45 a.m., Eleventh Marines, twin-engine Piper Seneca, two-seater, two civilian dead, no Marine injuries or deaths.* When I telephoned the base Public Affairs officer, Lt. Col. Gail Stienon tried to answer with a voice that hadn't yet warmed up to the idea of talking.

Lieutenant Colonel Stienon was a woman powerful in rank and stature, brusque at all times, and with a thick New England accent she hadn't let go of despite worldwide tours of duty. "Whatcha got?"

I told her about the plane crash. The tent city. The two dead civilians.

"Write up a release . . . call me back, and make it quick."

"Yes, Ma'am."

Time, date, and place: the correct placement of information in a news release, following the actual incident, itself. I played around with the wording, crossed through a few dramatic phrases—save those for radio.

A few minutes later, I was reading the release over the telephone to her: "*A twin-engine Piper Seneca crashed into a tent city of Marines preparing for a routine training exercise, approximately 12:45 a.m., today, at Marine Corps Base, Camp Pendleton, California. Both pilot and passenger are confirmed dead. No Marine casualties have been reported at this time. Names of the dead are being withheld, pending notification of next of kin.*"

She sounded awake now. I tried to picture my boss as she must have looked sitting up in bed, her short salt-and-pepper pixie haircut flattened by a pillow on one side of her head, spiky

1. Tracy's father, Jim.

2. Tracy, four, with her two-year-old brother, Mike, and parents in 1963.

3. Tracy, five, with her three-year-old brother in 1964.

4. Tracy, first grade, 1965.

5. Major Woggon, a.k.a. the Silver Fox, promotes Tracy to sergeant in Okinawa, 1980.

6. Tracy, twenty-one, and six months pregnant with twins, at her Okinawan apartment, 1980.

7. Tracy celebrates Morgan's second birthday, 1982.

8. Tracy, twenty-four, a sergeant at Camp Pendleton in 1983.

9. Tracy, front and center, with her platoon at Quantico in 1985.

10. Col. John Hopkins in 1980 as the commanding officer of the Fifth Marine Regiment at Camp Pendleton. Courtesy of the Fifth Marine Regiment.

11. Tracy, twenty-seven, during the 1986 summer with General Hopkins.

12. Tracy, twenty-eight, on the morning in 1987 she was both promoted and fired.

13. Tracy, with her daughter, Morgan, in 2008 at Dodger Stadium.

on the other. "Change it," she was saying, "to . . . a *civilian* twin-engine Piper Seneca, blah, blah, blah . . . and then send it out."

I sent the release first to wire services, where the reporters on night duty nonchalantly took the information and asked me to spell my name twice so I could be quoted as the official base spokesperson. Then I called the local print media—the *Oceanside Blade-Tribune*, the *Los Angeles Times*, and the *San Diego Union*—whose reporters on night duty grabbed the news as if it were the last morning doughnut.

At home around eight that morning, after the Sunday duty had relieved me for his watch, my in-laws from Missouri called. "We just heard you on the radio," my mother-in-law said. "The plane crash . . . and how you said it was nothing short of a miracle that a forklift left beside a tent had spared the lives of so many sleeping Marines." Looking back, I am awestruck at the level of responsibility bestowed upon someone so young. When I look out onto the faces of my college students—so many of them dragging in weary from pulling an all-nighter—I am sometimes overwhelmed by a sense of sadness for them, even for my own thirty-year-old daughter long graduated from college. Morgan followed the plan I had for her, which included college immediately after high school. Had she wanted anything else? I don't know. The woman who was never given the option of college, until her early forties, was determined her daughter would have no other option.

During those days in the eighties, I also understand now how much I took for granted. My mother would often ring up from her five acres in Paradise: "I just saw you interviewed on television at the Beirut memorial service! Who was that poor sobbing Marine you had your arm around?" Or, "I just read what you said about that overturned tank last night and those poor decapitated Marines."

What you wouldn't have read in a Marine Corps press release

was how sand during desert training jammed most of the weapons or how many helicopters broke down during cold weather training at Bridgeport, California, or how the filters on most of our gas masks were old and leaking, and I found that as I was growing up in the Marines and as a Marine, I was sometimes looking for ways to rebel against the falseness that *Everything worked, The weather was fine, Everybody was happy to be here, Mission accomplished.*

Underneath the newspaper clippings in my footlocker are my sleeping bag, helmet, and gas mask, all gear that should have been turned in, but given the circumstances of my less-than-honorable departure, all but forgotten by some poor Supply clerk who probably had to fudge his records in a cover-up. And somewhere at the bottom of the footlocker, behind all this gear, are the sergeant insignia I used to pin to my shirt collars and an old pair of cammies I'm embarrassed to say my middle-aged thighs can barely squeeze into after all these years.

In anger over our divorce, Tom sold my dress blues and dress whites, but I've held onto the red-and-gold officer's bars and two dog tags on a silver chain, and a black-and-white photograph that captures Major Woggon promoting me to sergeant in Okinawa: I hadn't known until too late that the Silver Fox also had orders to Okinawa, arriving just one day ahead of us.

And there's a dull pair of once spit-shined boots and a colorful row of ribbons and the medals and the weapons guides for the M60 machine gun and both howitzers and lesson guides from Quantico's Basic School on land navigation and Soviet tanks; and there's a paperback guide with first aid information such as start the breathing, stop the bleeding, and treat for shock; the Geneva rules for POW status, as well as a Marine's General Orders. Since my discharge, I've often tested my memory on the eleven General Orders. Why, I don't know, except that when I walk along the beach here in Florida, I sometimes mumble them under my breath. Doing so not only regulates my breathing but preserves an odd sense of connection to the Marine Corps I'm still unable to sever: *To walk my post in a military manner, keeping always on the alert, and observing everything that takes place within sight or hearing.* More than twenty years since my discharge, the General Orders are as imprinted into the dendrites of my memory as O Positive within the metal of my dog tags.

All this in the footlocker, and the officer's sword with the ivory handle that I keep tucked under the bed as a weapon against possible intruders, I have safeguarded through household moves to and from Okinawa, from St. Louis to the Carolinas, and on to Florida. One day, Morgan, my only child, will marry and produce an heir to this footlocker miscellany.

There's one other item in my footlocker that should have been reclaimed the day I was discharged in April 1987. My green military ID card. I hate looking at it, and yet I can't not look whenever I come across it. It's like knowing I shouldn't stare at the twisted wreckage of the upside-down truck in flames on the side of the highway, but I can't help myself.

The laminate on the upper left corner of the ID card has now pulled apart from the back side. I've been tempted for years to peel away the layers of plastic and see myself in a way only the admin clerk who typed in the information has seen it: up close and personal on February 15, 1987. The same day I was promoted to chief warrant officer and then fired a half hour later.

Despite the peeling laminate, the card still appears official: the U.S. government seal is the same as the one on my passport. The expiration date, *Indefinite*, is considered a privileged status on ID cards for military officers. The normal identifiers are all typed in: DOB (date of birth), *590120*; hair, *Brown*; eyes, *Green*; height, *5'7"*; weight, *135*. That was a lie. I never got below 144 pounds the entire ten years I was a Marine despite running three to five miles a day, except those days or weeks I resorted to laxatives and diuretics.

Looking back, I see I probably should have waited the six months and joined the Navy. The Navy's weight standards would have allowed me to weigh in at a comfortable 160 for my height. But the Marines? Want to win a war? *Tell it to the Marines!* In the Marines, the maximum weight for my height was 144, and my body, even during boot camp, had refused to budge below it, at least not without resorting to life-threatening measures.

I hadn't thought of myself as being heavy during high school in the late seventies. I had shared bell bottoms and halter tops with all my girlfriends, who I never thought of as being overweight, and so I hadn't any concept of myself as being fat either. Too, like most girls, I suppose, I had a habit of seeing myself through the eyes of the boys who were interested in me, and there had been a football star or two, a baseball pitcher, the band's drum major, and in my senior year the married man to perpetuate the notion I was at least average.

When the Marine recruiter had said I needed to lose fifteen pounds before the Marines would consider me, I was embarrassed. For weeks afterward, I drank nothing but water and powdered protein shakes; even today, the grind of a blender recreates memories of self-depravation. By the end of three weeks, when I weighed close enough for orders to boot camp, I was also suffering from such a severe kidney infection that my doctor threatened to hospitalize me if I didn't quit the liquid protein diet and return to solid food.

To pile on more humiliation, at Parris Island in 1977, drill instructors weighed us every Friday, and every Friday I stepped on the scale and watched the DI's face screw itself into a mean caricature. She would announce to the other DIs: "She's *still* 144." And then there followed the usual barrage from all three: *You have to get five pounds below the maximum allowed weight! What's wrong with you?*

Don't you want to be a Marine? (I'd wanted to be a Marine bad enough to cheat my way in, I could have told them.)

No one seemed cognizant that my uniforms had been altered three times in eight weeks to accommodate my shrinking frame. I was losing inches, not pounds, or I was gaining muscle and losing fat, or whatever it is that happens to your body when you're running and marching all day, and given less than three minutes to wolf down a meal. But I was still a fat Marine according to the scale, and *fat* and *Marine* are two words as oxymoronic as *pretty ugly*. After Major Woggon jabbed his finger into my thigh years later, I bought every lotion and potion advertised to shrink thighs over the next ten years. I read *Thin Thighs in Thirty Days*, only to learn I was already doing more than the author recommended. Once, I even paid for an expensive herbal wrap that was guaranteed to shrink thighs two inches in an hour, and it worked, only they exploded back to original size by morning.

Years later, in 1986, when I was the Public Affairs officer of the New River Air Station, a sergeant in company admin, "the mole," called one Friday afternoon and tipped me off, and I'm sure every other woman on her underground list, to the surprise weigh-in the company commander had scheduled for Monday morning. On my home scales that night, I weighed five pounds over: the penalty would be public humiliation with remedial physical training and a career-ending reference in my service record book.

Under my sink was the stash of blue laxative pills and boxes of diuretics for just such an emergency. By now I knew the routine. Every four hours, I filled a glass from the tap, popped out a laxative from the crackly packaging and then a diuretic tablet, and gulped both in a single swallow. In the mirror, the twenty-six-year-old woman looking back was beginning to look less and less like the woman I thought she should have become by now. She had climbed from the rank of private to earn a commission as an officer. She gave orders, commanded the attention of senior officers during staff meetings, and was the second fastest woman runner on base, but she couldn't control the argument in her brain that screamed she still wasn't good enough—had even cheated her way into the Marines and, therefore, would never be as good as anyone else.

Later that evening when I spoke with my mother by telephone, I had explained my fears at being caught overweight at the Monday weigh-in. She wanted to know what Tom had to say about me taking laxatives and diuretics.

"I guess he's gotten used to it, by now."

She sighed. "They're going to kill you."

I could have laughed. As if death mattered. Death, I could accept. In all fairness, I couldn't blame the Corps. The ideal Marine was someone like Tom: lean and wiry, someone who could easily wiggle under concertina wire, who could be tossed over a wall or buddy carried back to medics if injured. Body-building men or larger framed women like me were unsuitable on many levels, notwithstanding the Marine Corps' desire that each of us present a recruiting poster image.

So I had eaten nothing that weekend prior to the weigh-in, drank only water, popped laxatives, and even stopped drinking water after noon on Sunday. On Sunday afternoon, I went for a walk dressed in one of those plastic suits designed to make you sweat, and I carried in my hand a tiny package of tissues in case of an emergency, and halfway home I was running toward the woods for cover.

On Monday, I stepped on the scales at 138. I had lost nine

pounds in forty-eight hours. Of course, I knew it wasn't real, and had the company commander weighed me the next morning, the scales would have read a pound over my maximum and I would have suffered through remedial PT.

On the front of my ID card is an awkward looking signature. Can it really be mine? This controlled slanted loop with a hint of something Southern but so foreign from the nearly illegible way I have of signing my name today. On the card, the signature is a black scrawl of ink under my typed name, *Tracy Ellen*, along with Tom's last name—a German name that when Anglicized has an embarrassing pronunciation. When Morgan graduated from college and moved to Hollywood to pursue an acting career, she immediately dropped the last name.

And then, of course, there is the photograph on the ID card. The real reason I try to avoid looking at this thing. I'm twenty-eight. My hair is nearly shoulder-length in one of those spiral eighties' perms and at a length dangerously close to violating regulations. I'm wearing the olive-green woolly-pulley sweater with the shoulder and elbow patches, the style patterned after our British counterparts, over a khaki shirtwaist. On the collar are the new officer bars that Tom, aftershave fresh and smiling, had pinned on during the promotion ceremony. On my face is the saddened expression you might expect from a police mug shot: a similar distance, a lack of light behind the eyes, my mouth a long, flat line. The photo was taken ten minutes after I'd been fired.

One of my sergeants, Marie Flowers, had followed me to my car that morning as I was hauling the final box of personal effects from my office. "Why can't you just tell me what's going on, Ma'am? Why can't you tell us where you're going?"

I loaded the box and fought the temptation to slam the trunk. "Because I've been ordered not to talk about it, Marie."

In the interrogation room at Military Police Headquarters, the captain was lifting a long yellow sheet and folding it over the top for a fresh beginning. What I wouldn't give for a fresh start. And yet, this was a beginning of sorts. I couldn't imagine going back to being the Public Affairs officer for the New River Air Station after having been fired, whatever the conclusion of the investigation. There was no going back for a Marine threatened with a court-martial. A Marine accused of having an affair with a general. There could only be a plodding through, a head down and move on approach.

Tom had said that morning of the interrogation before backing down the driveway to take Morgan to school that we would make it through this. What had made him so hopeful? The summer before, he had crumbled when I said I wanted a divorce. I had asked for the divorce within two nights of returning from the eight-week course on mass communications that the Department of Defense sponsored at the University of Oklahoma. The separation had been hard on Tom, who struggled with being a single parent. He said it was always harder on the one left behind. And he was right.

We had been in bed, talking, when the words finally found their way from my mouth. Tom startled me by leaping from the bed and running from the room. I jumped up, grabbed a robe from the back of the chair across the room, and ran after him. I found him down the hall in Morgan's darkened bedroom. He was kneeling by the side of her bed, sobbing. I put my arms around him and helped him to his feet and then down the hall to our bedroom, and willed myself to be emotionally detached. I couldn't afford to retreat the ground I had gained. It was true I loved him, probably would forever, but for two months in Oklahoma, I had tasted a life free of his influence. At twenty-seven, I had discovered how it felt to manage my own money for the first time, and I was remembering how successful I could be as a student when I was free to study late into the night without the tug of someone pleading with me to come to bed.

And so, just as my parents had done in their late twenties, Tom and I separated. Morgan and I moved into a smaller house I could afford on my own, and Tom moved to the bachelor officers' quarters on base. For three months, we lived apart, although he called every day and made surprise visits to my office and house, until finally, at the end of the summer, after seeing the strain in his face as he stood on my porch, leaning down to kiss Morgan good night and then leaning toward me until I took a step backward, I finally relented to a reconciliation. And the next day, I admitted the reconciliation in a telephone conversation to a disappointed General Hopkins.

Surprisingly, I felt no sense of loss the day Tom moved back home, no sense of loss over the drawers in the bedroom dresser I was giving up again, nor over the loss of freedom in the house that had allowed me to come and go as I pleased. My husband was now home. I was resigned to what was best for Morgan.

We were moving forward, too. Life was okay and getting better each day. Full of happy gatherings with our friends again on Friday nights at our favorite Mexican restaurant. An intimate weekend at the beach where during a brisk fall sunrise we had sipped champagne from the bottle because I had forgotten to pack the glasses, and then we had made love under the blanket to the pounding of surf and the cries of sea gulls overhead. There had been the afternoon during which we taught Morgan to ride a bicycle and the Sunday afternoons curled up on the sofa to watch football games. The New Year's Eve where we held to our tradition of a midnight supper and lovemaking, ignoring the many invitations from friends.

And then came that awful day in February. I had been blindsided. After six months of reconciliation, I was compelled to open what I had locked away in a private chamber of my mind, compelled to confess to Tom the summer romance with General Hopkins.

The captain looked up from her notepad. "Are you going to tell me why you and your husband separated last summer?" She obviously wasn't satisfied with my earlier response about not wanting to discuss the personal details about my marriage.

I glanced out the window. An MP van was backing up, providing a view of my car. From the van, two military policemen exited from both sides. They were wearing cammies with black belts and pistols around their waists. The Marine who exited from the passenger side had said something to the driver, who answered with a pretend punch to his passenger's arm. They disappeared from view when they walked around the side of the building toward the main entrance.

The captain said, "Your husband is a captain, right?"

"Yes, Ma'am.

"Tracy," she said, "did you or did you not have an affair with General Hopkins last summer?"

Hearing the general's name brought a sudden reverence into the room I hadn't expected. The captain and I might have been secluded behind the heavy drapes of a confessional, the whir of the running cassette tape a willing priest. This was the moment

I had anticipated for two weeks, and yet I still couldn't determine how I should answer.

She was waiting, judging, evaluating my silence. I had no way of knowing how I would answer. I had forgotten about the torn seat fabric, so when I tried to cross my legs, I felt an undertow of snagged pantyhose.

"You must answer the question, or you will be held in contempt."

I set my foot back down. "I will neither confirm nor deny any relationship with General Hopkins."

The captain sat taller, surprised to find herself in checkmate. She twirled her pen furiously in and around her fingers. I wanted to snatch it from her and slam it on the desk.

"You'll be in contempt . . ."

"Then *charge* me, Captain, my answer will not change." She had to notice my lip quivering if I could feel it, the little muscles puckering involuntarily as if my chin had a string that was being tugged up and down.

"One more time, for the record, did you and Hopkins fraternize?"

"And one more time for the record, Captain, I will neither confirm nor deny any relationship with General Hopkins."

★

When I met John Hopkins in 1981, he was a colonel with a reputation for chewing up and spitting out Marines the way he did the butt end of his cigar. In his younger years, in 1956, he had been the tall, broad-shouldered football team captain for Navy. In the early eighties, he commanded the Fifth Marine Regiment, the Corps' most highly decorated combat unit.

"There's no way Hopkins will ever allow a woman Marine reporter to cover his regiment," my Public Affairs officer had said, shaking his head. But I had been relentless. I pleaded until he finally said it couldn't hurt to make a phone call, and I ran from his office to the telephone on my desk in the pressroom.

By then, I was twenty-two and a new mother, and Tom and I were at Camp Pendleton. But after only six months I had grown bored with reporting on Officers' Wives Club teas, Navy Relief Fund drives, and Pet-of-the-Week features. Here, I hadn't been allowed to cover infantry training as I had in Okinawa. A couple of years earlier, seven women had sued the *New York Times* for the same type of discrimination. The bastion of all newspapers had the audacity to advertise for and categorize jobs as *male* and *female* until a river of unrest among its savviest women reporters rose up to demand change.

I didn't know all this back then. I wish I had. I wasn't savvy enough to stay on top of current events, for had I armed myself with the news that the *New York Times* had been compelled to change its policy toward women I could have aimed even higher, hoped for even more change within the Marine Corps.

I was hungry for an assignment of importance, something with teeth to it, when I made up my mind to be assigned to Fifth Marines as Hopkins's beat reporter so I could cover the colonel's upcoming combat exercise in the Mojave Desert at Twentynine Palms. The "colonel's war" some called it. I was still trying to prove something, although what it was I couldn't yet name. I wasn't conscious of anything, other than of not wanting to end my military career unfulfilled, my purpose undetermined or unrealized.

The sergeant major for Fifth Marines had placed me on hold to check the colonel's schedule. I tried to imagine the colonel's reaction. On May 15, 1975, Hopkins had been among a company of Marines sent in by President Ford to rescue a U.S. Merchant ship, the *Mayaguez*, from the Khmer Rouge. Before that, he had been on special assignment in Cambodia and had taken part in the evacuation of the Cambodian capital, Phnom Penh. But in 1981 he was a recent widower, having lost his wife suddenly to a brain aneurysm. In the late seventies, Hopkins had been a lieutenant colonel when he made *Newsweek* and *Time* magazine headlines for his off-base brawling in the bars around Oceanside. He and another Marine officer had been walking shore patrol when a group of Vietnam War protestors shouted at them, *Baby killers!* Everyone assumed the negative publicity would wash up John's chances for bird colonel, but he had earned a Silver Star in Vietnam for bravery, a Bronze Star as well, and so generals whitewashed the "conduct unbecoming an officer" with a letter of reprimand rather than convene a court-martial.

Truth is, John Hopkins had a reputation for doing everything the hard way. He had earned the Silver Star at thirty-one. *They* said Marines ever decorated with a Medal of Honor or Silver Star who live are really dead inside: half-numb from shock, half-crazed to prove they deserve to live at all.

The sergeant major was back on the phone. "The colonel will see you at 1500."

I looked at my watch, stunned and unprepared for a meeting in less than an hour. And my clothes. I was wearing a short-sleeved khaki shirt, olive-drab skirt, and black pumps. Not the combat boots and camouflage uniform I should be wearing to meet an infantry officer like Colonel Hopkins. But I couldn't turn the opportunity down for fear there might never be another, so I told the first sergeant I would be delighted to the meet the colonel at 1500.

"*Delighted!* This ain't no kind of tea party you're coming to, Sergeant. You better not pull that kind of crap talk with John Hopkins, you hear me, Marine?"

Click. Silence. The shaking spread from my hands to a fluttering in my gut. I had blown it with the sergeant major, and being dressed as I was in a froufrou uniform, not boots and cammies as a war hero would expect of someone requesting to be the regiment's beat reporter, meant I was sure to blow it with the colonel as well.

Best I can remember, the headquarters building of Fifth Marines was a white, board-sided building on a sloping California hillside. It's gone now, so I'm told, or converted to something altogether different and benign. But that day, the warm April breezes fluttered through the regiment's red-and-gold flag and caused the tethering cables to clang furiously against the flagpole.

Inside the paneled waiting room, I looked over the trophies of sports victories, citations of valor, and the rows of grim faces, all previous commanders framed in black-and-white history. A Pfc. in starched cammies and mirror-like boots stepped into the lobby from behind a door, took my name, and disappeared again. As I waited, I followed the chain of faces on the wall to their strongest living link and searched for something like understanding for my skirt and high heels in the eyes of Col. John Hopkins. His were deep-set eyes, not large, but not small either. And there was the firmness of his face, chiseled along the jaw by a lineage so Caesar, so warring that it seemed set as if just ending a command. On his chest were the medals and, of course, the Silver Star.

"Sergeant, they will see you now."

I followed the Pfc. down a hallway and noticed that Marine admin clerks, all men, had stopped typing and were glancing around office partition walls as we passed.

The Pfc. led me into a room that was heavily furnished. Flags stood in one corner; in front of the large desk, two chairs were positioned at forty-five-degree angles to one another. There were framed photos on the wall. To the rear of the office, a door that led outside, and in the doorframe someone large was leaning, giving the appearance of being half in, half out, uncertain.

The Pfc. announced my name and scurried off. Another figure I hadn't noticed moved from the rear of the office and into the center of the room. This shorter man in sharply creased cammies with polished black boots and a shiny bald head had sleeves rolled above his elbows. His forearms were tattooed with the Marine emblem of eagle, globe, and anchor. On his collar were sergeant major rank insignia.

"Colonel," he said, turning to the dark figure in the doorway, "this is the sergeant from Public Affairs who wants to cover the Fightin' Fifth."

The figure leaning in the doorway straightened. He walked forward, and I recognized the deep-set eyes and the firm, square jaw from the photograph in the outer office, the silver wings of a colonel's rank insignia. His handshake was warm, firm, but tender; mine felt sweaty in comparison.

His voice, the smoothness of an alto sax, was deliberate, confident. "You want to cover the regiment." Neither a question nor a statement. He leaned overhead now, closer for my answer, and was still slowly shaking my hand. In his creased camouflage of earthy greens and browns, I was placing him among redwoods in ancient forests.

"Yes, Sir."

He released my hand. "Why?"

"*Why?*"

"Why!"

I launched into everything I remembered from a half-hour's worth of research on the regiment, its illustrious battle at Belleau Wood . . .

"Sir, today's stories about the regiment are important to the public. They demonstrate the Corps' level of combat readiness to members of Congress, and to the Marines of the Fifth, and to hometowns all across America . . ."

I had taken the tone of a politician on a stumping mission. He appeared to have lost interest, turning away to settle into the leather chair behind the desk. I remained standing, quiet.

"Have you ever fired a weapon, Sergeant?"

"No, Sir." Surely he had known only women military police fired weapons. It would be four years later before weapons firing would be added to women's recruit training at Parris Island.

He turned to the sergeant major. "I'm supposed to allow a woman in the field with my Marines, and to make matters worse, a woman who's never fired a weapon?"

The sergeant major stepped forward, blocking my vision of the colonel and his of me. "Colonel, I don't like the idea any more than you do, Sir."

They were reminding me of everything I was not—this Marine who had cheated her way into their Corps—and I felt exposed, naked, a fraud.

"Colonel," said the sergeant major, "what if we said she had to be weapons qualified, with the M-16?" The sergeant major turned toward me, possibly searching for a reaction. I felt the flush of embarrassment. All three of us knew I wouldn't be allowed on a rifle range.

The colonel rose from behind the desk. "I like that idea, Sergeant Major." And to me, "Sergeant, you have three weeks to get assigned somehow to the rifle range. If you qualify with the M-16, you can accompany us to Twentynine Palms. If you can't, tell your Public Affairs officer to send us a Marine who can. Roger that?"

"Yes, Sir."

And that was that. My first meeting with Col. John Hopkins. He had cracked a door in the rigid exterior of Marine Corps tradition. Whether he meant to do so is doubtful, looking back. I imagine he never thought he would see me again as I thanked him for the audience and made a daring about-face in pumps, marching from his world, wincing at my clicking heels, and hoping against all hope my rear end wasn't swinging like one of those saloon doors you see in Westerns. But I left thinking he had delivered a challenge, and where there was a challenge, there was hope for a victory. His word that afternoon was final; I could accept that. I could also accept his word would be honored, although the rest was not entirely up to me.

"Who do you think you are?" yelled Master Gunnery Sergeant Dale Hunter, Vietnam veteran and the senior enlisted Marine at Public Affairs, when I requested orders to the rifle range. "I couldn't put a rifle in your hands if I wanted to."

"C'mon, Top, Colonel Hopkins is actually giving me a chance. We've never been able to get a woman in the field overnight."

"Had plenty of them in Vietnam."

"They were civilians, Top. Civilian journalists and a few nurses."

Three days and a few phone calls later, Top came through with orders to send me to the rifle range.

The alarm clock rang at 4:00 a.m., but I was already awake. I hadn't been able to sleep; I was too afraid of oversleeping and missing the cattle car that was to transport the entire rifle range detail from the armory to the firing range.

Tom rolled over. "What time is it?"

"Four."

"I don't know why you're doing this to yourself."

"Go back to sleep. I've reset the clock for five thirty."

I dressed in cammies and boots. Brushed my teeth. Washed my face. I considered dabbing on foundation, but what was the point? I swiped on black mascara, the waterproof brand that holds up on five-mile runs as well as through the tear-gas chamber I had to endure once a year.

When I was ready to leave for the armory, I nudged Tom awake.

"Morgan's clothes are laid out for you." He mumbled something incoherent.

At 5:00 a.m., the armory enclosed with prison-like fencing and concertina wire was brightly lit. Marines in line were keeping warm either by breathing into cupped hands or by smoking. Some, in the shadows of the cattle car trucks, took advantage of the semi-darkness to stuff their hands into pockets. I walked toward the end of the line with my ID card in my hand. No one seemed particularly surprised to see a woman, but then it was early and everyone appeared tired as they shuffled closer to the window where the armorer was passing out weapons and gear.

"Military Police?" he said, when I handed over my ID.

"Public Affairs."

He scanned the list on his clipboard, found my name, disappeared behind metal racks, and emerged with an armload of gear. He handed me an M-16 rifle, a sling, two empty magazine cartridges, some sort of utility belt, ear plugs, a nail (a nail?), and a scoring book.

"Good luck."

At the rifle range, we lined up by the ammunition truck for our boxes of live ammo. A staff sergeant divided us into two details. Alpha detail, mine, was to fire first; bravo detail, he sent to the targets behind the berms two hundred yards from the closest firing line. These men acted as if they knew the routine, and why wouldn't they have? They had been qualifying once a year since boot camp. But when the two details split for opposite directions, mine for the line, I felt lost.

"What's the matter?" asked the staff sergeant. "Lost?"

"I've never done this before."

"You've never been to the rifle range?"

"No, Sir."

He lifted his cover from his head and ran a hand through the stubble and then refitted the cover to his head. "Christ, they've sent me a Marine who's never fired a goddam rifle?" He looked downrange for a moment.

"Go pick out a firing station and sit your ass down. And don't touch your ammunition until I tell you to, you hear me?"

"Yes, Sir."

I went to the only firing station that was still available, and, imitating the other Marines around me, sat cross-legged. Across my lap the rifle felt like a heavy plastic toy, and thinking it so, I felt a flush of guilt. Marines have a creed about their rifles: *This is my rifle. There are many like it, but this one is mine. My rifle is my best friend. It is my life. I must master it as I must master my life. My rifle without me is useless. Without my rifle, I am useless. I must fire my rifle true. I must shoot straighter than my enemy who is trying to kill me. I must shoot him before he shoots me.* I must have heard various lines of this chanted more than a dozen times by male recruits at Parris Island. With shaved heads and thumping boots, they marched with a singleness of purpose past our girlish platoon as we were being marched toward classrooms for lessons on how to properly apply makeup or on how to coordinate the color of lipstick and nail polish with the scarlet cording on our headgear. The men marching in the opposite direction past our platoon knew what they were being trained for. War. I wasn't exactly sure what I and the other women of my platoon were being trained for—our World War II sisters would have shouted to *Free a Man to Fight!*—but I remember thinking as I watched those recruits trample by, men who hadn't seen a woman in several months, men with fixed stares and rifles in their hands, that whatever they sprinkled on food at Parris Island to turn a teenager into someone who was willing to die for his country was working.

Halfway down the rifle range firing line, the staff sergeant was speaking with a Marine in a tower. The staff sergeant looked up and down the line until he found me, and pointed. Both men shook their heads. Minutes later, he was standing at my firing station.

"Let's talk about the definition of live ammo." He kneeled and picked up my boxes of ammunition and the two magazines. "Always, always, *always* keep this weapon pointed downrange. Okay, what did I just say?"

"You said, always keep the weapon pointed downrange."

"No . . . I said always, always, *always* keep it pointed downrange. Do you know what happens to Marines who forget, Sergeant?"

"No, Sir."

"They get shot! That's right, I'm going to shoot and kill the Marine who forgets and turns a weapon in any other direction than downrange at his target. Do you hear me, Sergeant?"

"Yes, Sir."

"Don't call me Sir."

"Yes, Staff Sergeant."

"Load your magazines."

I pulled a brass round from one of the cardboard boxes of ammo and wedged it into the magazine.

"Not like that! You're going in backward!"

He snatched the magazine and used the tip end of another bullet to free the jammed round. He loaded ten and handed me the magazine. He showed me how and where to load the magazine into the rifle, the location of the safety, how to know when the safety was on and off, when it should be on or off, and how to change direction of the scope with the nail.

When he was satisfied with his crash course, he waved at the Marine in the tower, who shouted: "All ready on the left? All ready on the right? All ready on the firing line! You may commence firing."

Through earplugs, the gunfire sounded like tinny blasts. The acrid odor of gun smoke filled the morning air. I stared through the scope at the white target with its black lines. I held my breath, as the staff sergeant instructed, and pulled back the trigger. Unprepared for the recoil, the rifle butt slammed into my right shoulder, and I felt my grip loosen on the weapon as if it were about to fly from my hands. When I grabbed control, I accidentally squeezed the trigger, sending another round downrange while my target was still down.

"Jesus!" the staff sergeant shouted. "Give them time to find your *first* shot."

"Sure thing, Staff Sergeant." My target popped into view. A white disk on a wooden pole waved left to right.

"Clean miss," he said behind me. "That means you missed the whole target. You probably hit Smitty's . . . Smitty, did she hit your target?"

Smith, a corporal, was bent over his rifle in a tight sitting position. He relaxed enough to let his head lift above the scope and grinned. "Don't know, Staff Sergeant, but I could always use a little extra help."

At the two hundred, I couldn't hit the target. I don't know where the bullets ended up. I had heard that bullets shot into the air have to land somewhere, so I wondered what was on the other side of the grassy berm beyond the targets. A pasture of dead cattle? Horses running for the barn? A cursing farmer on a tractor? All I knew for certain was that beneath the berm were hidden Marines who were pulling down our targets, spotting the hits with disks, hoisting targets back into the air, and then indicating the exact location by pointing to it with the wooden pole so we, the shooters, could mark our scores.

Although I couldn't hit my target, I could hit others. When my round splintered a target's wooden frame with a *ziiiiiiii-ziiiiiiing*, someone screamed *Sonavobitch!* from behind the berm. At other times, puffs of dirt rose on the hill above my target, an indicator that my shots were too high. The coaching from the staff sergeant had gone a little like this:

Elevation, two clicks right. Fire when ready.

No, too far. One click back.

Lift your muzzle for Pete's sake.

What did you do wrong that time, huh? HUH? You breathed, didn't you? What did I tell you about breathing? No breathing! Goddam it, woman, will you just listen to me?

Okay, pick up your shit and move it back to the three hundred.

On the first round at the three hundred, I hit the target, *my* target.

"Sweet Jesus, that's what *I'm* talking about," said the staff sergeant. "Okay now, you got a feel for it, right? Check your wind direction."

I glanced left and right at the corners of the berms to see the play of wind in the flags. "It's picked up. I'm rotating windage a click."

"Look who's getting cocky all of a sudden."

I formed my shoulder around the butt of the rifle, rested my elbow on the inside of my left knee, and sighted in at the black ring below the bull's-eye. I exhaled, held it, held it, and squeezed. The target went down, a good sign someone down there thought he saw a shot go through paper. I waited. The target popped up with a black disk in the middle of the bull's-eye.

"Yes!" I said. But when I looked behind me for the staff sergeant, he was already walking down the line, stopping to give pointers along the way. He glanced back and made a pointing gesture downrange that said, *Get it done!* At the five hundred, I lay in the dirt, rifle buried against my shoulder, navel pressed into the earth, and squeezed the trigger. Another bull's-eye.

The next four days are a fuzzy memory of dark morning rides to the rifle range, of ricocheting bullets, and gun smoke. My scores increased each day, and on the last, Friday, several Marines cheered when my final score was announced: expert.

"You know," said the staff sergeant while I was waiting my turn to board the cattle car on that last afternoon, "you could probably make the Marine Corps rifle team with the way you've taken to it." But I had another plan.

The following Monday, I dressed in cammies and spit-polished boots. I pinned the expert badge to my chest, and seeing it there as I checked my reflection in the dresser mirror gave me pride. The rifle range experience had changed me. I had learned how to fieldstrip a rifle to its core. I could fire it with precision. I had mastered the rifle even if I hadn't mastered the juggling act of marriage, motherhood, and Marine Corps career.

I drove to Fifth Marines that Monday morning to show Colonel Hopkins my expert rifle badge. Somewhere along the way, I decided that the true Marine wasn't the man or woman who has killed or has even been trained to kill. The true Marine is the man or woman who pledges to live a life on the altar of sacrifice.

In Colonel Hopkins's paneled office that day, the sergeant major spoke first.

"Looks like we've got a woman reporter, Colonel."

Colonel Hopkins leaned back in his leather chair, glanced from my face to my left breast where I had pinned on the expert rifle badge, and then back to me.

"Expert, huh?"

"Yes, Sir."

"I'll be damned."

Then he smiled. And that was my second meeting with the colonel.

★

Colonel Hopkins and two battalions of Fifth Marines beat me to Twentynine Palms by a week. My orders were to fly in during the second week of the operation when there would be more newsworthy portions of the exercise to cover.

The night before my flight to the Mojave Desert, I was packing the 782 gear of helmet, gas mask, sleeping bag, poncho, poncho liner, two canteens, and canteen covers on loan from Supply at Fifth Marines. Spread across the bed were uniforms, underwear, cameras, lenses, film, and a small stack of Steno notebooks.

"Why are you doing this?" Tom asked, retrieving the gas mask that had slipped from the bed to the floor.

"It's my job, you know that."

"No, it's not your job . . . you volunteered for this. What about Morgan?" he said, as if believing he could use our daughter as the trump card.

I continued to pack in silence. And in the morning when it was time for me to leave, he hugged and kissed me as if he were afraid it might be the last time. And I suppose in a way that life-changing experiences have on us, it was.

I exited the C-130 plane to dry desert heat that pricked my skin with the feeling of a thousand needles, and I squinted against the glare of desert sun on sand at what little I could make out of the Corps' largest base. At nearly six hundred thousand acres, Twentynine Palms is three-fourths the size of Rhode Island.

A private was running toward me on the tarmac and said he

was assigned to drive me to the regiment's camp. We were tossing my gear into a jeep when a second lieutenant, loaded down with his ruck, said he needed a ride to the regiment. He ordered me to the back seat. When the private rolled his eyes, I shook my head as a warning.

There are no roads to a camp in the desert. We rolled over dunes and crashed so hard on the downside of sharp rocks that gear bounced from the jeep. The private and I leaped out and retrieved everything; the lieutenant remained in his seat, except for the two times we had to stop when he needed to relieve himself. It was then I wondered where I would go. I had not given much thought to there being no facilities, not even porta-johns.

The camp was a tent city in variegated shades of brown camouflage netting like spider webbing cast over trucks, helicopters, and tanks to blend them into the terrain from make-believe enemy air attacks. We rolled to a stop and the lieutenant jumped into the dust cloud overcoming our jeep. He ordered his gear unloaded.

A corporal ran forward, shouting to me above the whirring of a helicopter on a hill to the west. "Are you the sergeant from Public Affairs?"

I nodded.

"Follow me to that helicopter. The colonel's up there waiting for you . . . wants to give you an aerial tour of the operation."

I glanced back at the lieutenant, whose gaping mouth looked like a dust trap.

I climbed aboard the Huey. Colonel Hopkins was in headset already and handed one to me. I signaled a thumbs up when I heard his voice and those of the pilot and copilot above the propeller noise, trying hard to look as if I did this sort of thing every day. A crew chief strapped a belt around my waist; he hooked the metal clip at the far end into a ring bolted to the floor as a safety precaution in the event I fell out of my seat.

The rear of the helicopter lifted upward and the nose dipped forward as we soared over the camp. The colonel's voice crackled in my ears, and I strained to understand him the same way I struggle to make out blasted words from drive-through speakers at fast food joints.

Over an adjacent mountain range peppered with sagebrush, a tank column came into view, moving, according to the colonel, into position for the next day's firing exercise. We passed a CH-46 midair, and its crew chief, bravely kneeling in the open doorway, saluted.

The colonel briefed me on flank movements and fields of fire, all combat warfare talk that, unfortunately, I wouldn't truly understand until five years later during officer training at Quantico. When he talked about the tanks, I tried to remember something I had heard about the Third Army's tanks in *Patton*, hoping to reply with something intelligent. Thankfully, I can't remember the comment. Still, if the colonel felt cheated by my lack of combat experience, he never let on.

That hot dry night, I slept on the desert floor with my boots on after having been warned by the others about rattlesnakes and scorpions. I was the only woman surrounded by nearly a thousand men. I never slept. I looked into starlight that seemed brighter over the desert than anywhere else I'd ever been. I thought of my daughter's mobile that tinkled "Fly Me to the Moon" with its twirling miniature airplanes in an orbit above her crib. I craved her milky breath, her pudgy arms and legs crammed into a footed sleeper, her delicate fingers wrapped around a favorite blanket. She was eighteen months old, and I was certain Tom was thinking I hadn't appreciated all we had been through. Maybe he was right. Maybe I was wrong to volunteer for the desert assignment with Colonel Hopkins's Fifth Marines, or for anything else in the future that would separate me from our daughter. Or maybe

I was too afraid of how much I loved Morgan, too afraid of suffocating her with my love as Tom was suffocating me with his.

Thankfully, the coolness of night in the Mojave Desert provided a respite from the bees that swarmed us all day for drops of moisture. Bees tried to sneak into our mouths, our eyes, into our food, and into water canteens. At chow the first night, a Marine nearly choked on a bee.

Despite my memories of the heat, I don't remember sweating. The dry air seemed to suck away body moisture before it had time to make itself noticeable, or to activate a cooling sensation. I rarely had to face the toilet situation until after midnight either. The first night had been the scariest. I had fumbled for the e-tool within my pack, the device used to dig small trenches, and then I had stumbled away from the base camp and the sleeping Marines. Walking out into the rocky, dusty wilderness conjured the image of a lunar walk.

When I felt reasonably safe from discovery, I did it. Then like a good Marine, I buried it.

We ate our meals from cans of c-rations. I learned to swap most anything for beans and franks. I discovered how to make a tiny stove with a can and a burn tablet. The grunts shared their favorite recipes for what could be added to canned chicken to make a casserole. Even canned eggs were edible with enough Tabasco sauce.

The day I spent with second battalion, Marines shouted, *Make me a star!* hoping their faces and names would make it into their hometown newspapers. I was no longer *Hey Sergeant!* I had become *Desert Fox*, and I wasn't sure whether it was a sexual implication or a reference to World War II German field marshal Erwin Rommel, whose combat strategies in North Africa were legendary. Was my female presence an epic threat?

In the early evenings before sunset, I hopped aboard a Huey

for a twenty-minute flight to the main airfield of Twentynine Palms, where a tent city had all the conveniences of camp store, toilets, and showers, although I never took a shower. To do so would have seemed traitorous. I straggled into the head there one night to use the toilet before boarding the helicopter, looking more like a desert rat than fox, and found two women in fresh uniforms and a cloud of sweet body lotion, pinning up their wet braided hair. They looked me up and down. I smiled, and disappeared behind a stall door. I envied their cleanliness, but I didn't feel as if I belonged there with them. I belonged in the desert with the dust, the heat, the scorpions, the bees, the Marines, and Colonel Hopkins.

"Who is that?" one of them whispered. I didn't hear the response, if there was one, above the boot shuffle across the concrete floor and swoosh of the door.

My rolls of film and handwritten releases went into plastic baggies that I handed over to helicopter or C-130 pilots who flew each night to Camp Pendleton and returned in the morning. The plan was that someone in Public Affairs would meet the evening flights and retrieve the work. One evening after sending off news releases and canisters of film, I bought bottles of Tabasco and several cases of soda from the camp store on the advice from a seasoned Public Affairs officer, who told me to take something back to the troops from the rear whenever possible. I filled a five-gallon water jug with as much ice and sodas as it would hold, asked a couple of Marines from the store to help me load everything onto the Huey, and once we landed back at the regiment, I encouraged everyone to help themselves. I sensed I was fitting in. Doing my part. Belonging. Nothing seemed more important in that moment than being accepted by them.

They had a funny way of showing it, but they liked me. One

night, after a soda and Tabasco run, I decided to take a quick wash under camouflage netting. I asked two Marines to keep others away. They assured me they would. I stripped off dusty clothing, filled my helmet with water from a five-gallon can, and drenched myself from head to toe. The desert dirt made muddy rivers along my breasts, arms, and legs. Water trickled down my unshaven legs that felt warm and thick with hair. I was thankful my period had postponed its arrival, although I had packed for it.

In the middle of bathing, someone sounded the alarm for gas. Tear gas. We had been gassed, apparently, as part of the exercise. My head covered in soapy water, my body still wet and naked, I fumbled for my gas mask. After setting the seal, I slipped on a T-shirt and listened for an all clear. Nothing. I stepped outside the netting and was greeted by a hillside of Marines—mask free—whooping and cheering at my nearly nude presence in a gas mask. The scream inside the mask sounded oddly like someone else's. I ducked behind flimsy webbing and dressed with shaky fingers.

Several days had passed since I had last seen Colonel Hopkins. He was doing his job; I was doing mine. On day three, orders came for me to meet up with a tank battalion and ride aboard a tank. The ride to the tank encampment came via a jeep column that slithered like a slow moving rattlesnake through the desert. Each jeep sported a 50-caliber machine gun that took up most of the room in the rear. Two lance corporals in charge of my vehicle advised me to ride standing up, holding onto the machine gun in the firing position. I felt a little silly and declined. I squeezed in behind the cannon. We hit a rut and out I bounced onto the sharpest rock in the desert. The rest of the way I rode as they had suggested, clutching the machine gun and swiveling left and right with each sharp turn.

It was dark before we reached the tank encampment. Someone

shouted, "What do you mean there's a woman Marine here?" and, "Who the hell sent me a woman Marine?"

A lieutenant colonel, one of Hopkins's commanders, stepped into the dusty light stream of jeep headlights and nearly into my face. A crowd was surrounding us. "You see that five-ton, Sergeant?"

I squinted into the darkness for a truck with a covered canvas top, and nodded. "Yes, Sir."

The commander's hand darted to the right, seizing a chest full of uniform that belonged to a Pfc. "Pull that tailgate down!" he ordered. The Pfc. jumped toward the truck. He unhitched the tailgate and lowered it.

The commander pointed to the truck. "Sergeant, that tailgate is where you're sleeping tonight." He grabbed another Marine. "And you're going to guard her. No goddam woman Marine is going to get my ass in a sling. Good night!"

On the final day of the desert exercise, the "war," Marines moved into choreographed positions. I rode along in a lead tank, thankful not to be following our dust cloud. From my seat in the tank's popped hatch, I snapped photos of Cobra attack helicopters as they whirled by.

The tank's driver waved my attention toward a jeep racing for our tank. As it pulled alongside, the captain in the passenger seat yelled above the roar of our tank and the helicopters overhead, "Sergeant, you're coming with me." And then he pointed to the highest mountain in view. "The colonel wants you to see the war from up there."

We crested the hill and halted a number of yards away from the colonel's position so as not to overcome him with our dust cloud. The captain motioned for me to join the colonel and then drove back down the hill.

I found Colonel Hopkins sitting in an honest-to-God director's chair. He was dressed in a fresh uniform and clean black boots, and he did not acknowledge me at first. He appeared to be concentrating on the muffled sputtering of voices from a radio on a table beside him. When the radio was silent, I stepped forward and announced myself.

He greeted me with a smile and a sweep of his right arm. "What do you think of my war?"

"Impressive, Sir."

Below us was a smaller mountain range that engulfed a valley dotted with tanks and troops. Along the outer fringes aircraft gunships hovered with machine guns and live ammo. Paramount Pictures executives would have salivated over just such a movie set. This was make-believe war. What we couldn't have known that day was that in ten years, in a desert in the Middle East, *General* Hopkins would have to orchestrate Marine infantry in the ground war of Desert Storm, and I, a civilian, would receive a telephone call from my mother the night the first bombs dropped over Baghdad. "I know you feel you should be there," my mother will say. "I'll take care of Morgan if you feel you should go." I will hang up and cry. I will cry because for the first time I will choose my daughter over my sense of duty. And I will cry because I think my mother, for the first time in my life, understands who I am.

But this isn't 1991 yet, and Colonel Hopkins and I are still on a high, dusty mountain in the Mojave Desert. I was sliding off my helmet to use it as a makeshift seat beside him as he was reaching to the ground for his canteen cup. That's when I noticed the swarm of bees, yellow jackets, or sweat bees that encircled the rim of his cup. Their feathery wings like a buzzing chorus line jostled for positions on a limited stage.

I wish I could recall what I asked Colonel Hopkins up there on the mountain; I found it nearly impossible to take my eyes off the bees and off the square angle of his jaw as it moved when he issued commands to those on the desert floor below us. When he reached for his canteen cup, the humming mass of black-and-yellow bees divided, scrambling to either side of his hand. They crowded along the upper crest of the cup as he drank, and when he returned the canteen cup to the ground, the bees jockeyed back along the lip of the cup, filling the void left by the removal of his hand. I had never witnessed such power from one person. This man with a medal to prove he'd beaten death in the jungles of Vietnam had conquered nature, and me, as well.

★

After the Mojave Desert operation, John Hopkins had called me at Public Affairs to express his appreciation and admiration over the coverage. Several years later, when I was promoted to warrant officer, he had called again to offer congratulations. The first time we reunited in a face-to-face meeting, beyond exchanged glances at an officers' reception for the commandant, wasn't until the summer of 1986 at a change of command ceremony at Camp Lejeune. By then, Tom and I were separated and had been living apart for several weeks.

I had seen John at the change of command ceremony before he'd seen me. He was wearing cammies and boots and talking to Gen. Al Gray, who was in charge of the Second Marine Division and who shortly afterward became commandant. John spotted me and was soon standing dangerously close to me, close enough to start rumors. His aide, a fresh-faced second lieutenant, respectfully backed out of earshot. I should have taken a step backward, but I held my ground with the general, aware that my high heels were slowly sinking into the hot black asphalt.

Above the band's military march music, General Hopkins shouted, "Good to see you after all these years, Tracy. I hear you're a fine officer. You've made a lot of sacrifices along the way and they're paying off."

The band's bass drummer seemed to have caught up to my heartbeat. "I have you to thank, General—for opening the door for me."

Even John's attempts at lightness always carried the undertones of intensity. "I'd say you busted it down."

I suppose John could have been right, but I would always give him credit for having kept his word and taking me to the desert. What had he seen in me that day in his office when he challenged me to qualify with a rifle? If I had been a man, I might have interpreted his actions like those of a football coach who takes away a starting position from a lazy quarterback for the purpose of humiliating and motivating him toward regaining his status as a starter. And certainly John, as a football lineman and captain for Navy, and later a combat leader, knew about motivating a team to victory. But what had he seen in me? Desperation to measure up? And, if so, against whose near-impossible standard? His? Or mine?

After John's desert operation at Twentynine Palms in 1981, I had volunteered for every tough story assignment. I couldn't see it then, but with each separation from my family, I was driving a deeper wedge between Tom and me. In 1983 I had pleaded for orders to Beirut, but had been turned down. Military women weren't being allowed overseas, I was told—too dangerous. When I saw a front-page photograph of Army women filling sandbags in Somalia, I dropped the newspaper on Top Hunter's desk. "The Army's sending women to Somalia. Why can't I get orders to Beirut?"

"The Marines won't ever send a woman into a combat zone," he said.

The best orders I could wrangle that year were for mountain warfare training in Bridgeport, California, with Seventh Marines, and this time, the need to prove myself nearly killed me.

In June 1983, while Sally Ride was blasting her way into space, I was climbing ten thousand feet above sea level to stand on a California snowcapped mountain with two hundred men of Col.

Hank C. Stackpole's Seventh Marines. I was twenty-four that day, and hemorrhaging, though I didn't understand the gravity of my situation at that point.

On the way to the top of the mountain, with each hot spill of blood between my legs, I was silently cursing my body. I was weaker than I'd been in days, and struggling to hold my place in the long, single file of Marines that snaked ahead of and behind me. Somewhere above us, Sally Ride was skyrocketing into history. I was forging my own: no other woman Marine had made this climb. But the sudden hot spurts of blood between my legs increased the fear I could no longer camouflage this secret. I glanced over my shoulder at the Marine behind me. His eyes were on the ground, and so I faced forward again, casually allowing the fingers of my right hand to sweep my crotch, which still felt dry. For insurance that morning, I'd stuffed my last clean towel, folded as small as possible, between my legs. Less than a half mile into the climb, the towel had begun to chafe those delicate folds of skin down there.

Another spill of blood. I gave thanks for the towel; the chafing would heal. Everything heals in time. I placed my boots in the trail the man ahead was leaving for me, and this concentration—this focus on reaching the top of the mountain with the others—began to replace the running script within my mind for how I would break the news to Tom that I'd miscarried, again.

The week before leaving for Bridgeport, California, a home pregnancy test verified the bittersweet news. Morgan was now three, and so the timing seemed ideal, although with the career I was building, I wasn't entirely sure how I felt about it. I hoped another child might solidify our marriage. Tom's fear of losing me, or most likely his fear of a second failed marriage, was causing him to become overly protective. "Please don't go tonight," he'd say after dinner as I straightened the kitchen before leaving for a night college class on base. "Wouldn't you rather stay here with Morgan and me?" And truth is, yes, I would have preferred staying home rather than driving back to base and sitting in a classroom for three hours studying economics or the Russian class that I finally dropped because Tom couldn't support the number of homework hours the course required of me, and I'd exhausted efforts at justification.

I had passed on college once, but even then, I recognized the class distinction others made between those who went to college—between officers, even warrant officers like Tom who rose through the ranks—and the enlisted people like me. I couldn't blame him. What I loved about my husband most, his sense of self-acceptance in the world, was what I lacked most and needed.

The night I packed for Bridgeport, and while Tom was on base pulling a twenty-four-hour duty and Morgan was at the sitter's, a searing pain in my lower gut caused me to double over. The sharpness forced me to draw in quick, short breaths. I wanted to lie down, but all my gear yet to be packed—the uniforms, toiletries, even a gas mask—was on the bed. I willed myself to the chair across the room and sank down, folding my arms and leaning over, applying pressure to my abdomen. I panted and groaned through the cramping of a long contraction. Was my body rejecting this baby, too? Within a few moments, the tightness, like a slow-opening fist, loosened its hold. I eased to my feet and paced the length of the carpeted bedroom. No pain. No cramping. I continued with my packing.

But later that evening, as I loaded the gear into the car, the pain returned, and this time so severe I felt as if I were being gutted. I doubled over and leaned against the side of the car. I pressed my arms into my abdomen and stifled a scream that would surely have aroused our neighbors next door and half the neighborhood. Then a sudden urge to push, as if my bowels were on the verge of explosion, sent me dashing for the bathroom. What plopped into the toilet with enough force to make my body feel vacuumed clean was a bloody fist-sized mass of tissue. "The baby," I heard myself say. "The baby."

For some time, I sat quiet on the toilet seat in a sort of memorial silence. What was I waiting for? A sign? A wave of remorse? A flood of tears? My instinct was to call Tom, but he would insist I go to the hospital. And why? I was not hemorrhaging this time. I peeked between my legs at the knot of tissue lying bloody in the bottom of the toilet, and was tempted to reach in. Instead, I flushed.

The next morning, however, I rode in a jeep convoy with Marines from the Seventh Regiment to the Mountain Warfare Training Center that extended over forty-six thousand acres within the Toiyabe National Forest at an elevation of 6,762 feet. In the winter, snows might reach six to eight feet, and Marines from bases on both coasts endured cold weather survival training in the event they were called to fight in such a climate. During summers, like this one, they honed skills in mountainous terrain, preparing them to fight in, say perhaps, Afghanistan. Just two months earlier, Reagan had declared the Soviets an "evil empire," and the Soviets retaliated, calling Reagan a liar and comparing him to Hitler. The Cold War was heating up, and so was military training in the United States.

We pulled up to the base camp, a city of tents in rows of military straightness spread over a plateau at the foot of the mountain. Across the road and straight down were the rapids; the roar filled up the pristine air thick with pine. Evergreens dotted the riverbanks, and the scene reminded me of a Thomas Cole painting.

As the only woman, I had my own tent under the camp's single light post, which was like having a bull's-eye drawn over the flap. I lifted the flap to the tent and tossed in my ruck. The shuffle of footsteps caused me to turn.

"I'm Corporal Gomez, your jeep driver," he said, and extended a hand. He was a lance corporal, and the corners of his mouth were lifting into a smile that faded quickly when the air was suddenly pierced with shouts for help. Corporal Gomez disappeared, and when I stepped outside, I saw him running toward the river below, merging with a herd of Marines who were kicking up an avalanche of shale, rocks, and dust. I grabbed a camera and ran after them, slipping and sliding fifty feet to the bottom.

By the time I reached the riverbank, two Marines had already strung a catch line cross the river. I went to work, squeezing off photographs, until I saw that wedged between boulders was the bare back of a man's body, face down. One of the two Marines working the catch line yelled, "He's dead all right. Blue as Christmas." When they had secured the line to both ends of the river, four Marines waded in with arms linked at the elbow. They shuffled left, then right, left and right until they reached the body. This was not my first dead body—I'd been fourteen when my grandmother died from breast cancer—but this was my first dead Marine, and I lowered the camera. This image would have to be mentally recorded, and I sensed that somehow we would all be changed by this, or at least I would be. I was nearly impatient to see the dead man's face, to catalog the moment, to feel the loss.

They lifted the dead Marine, turned him gently, and I finally saw his face. The eyes were open, fixed, as if he had been determined to face his fate, and his face was pale and horribly bloated. Someone behind me whispered the dead boy's name, and said he was from Colorado and that today was his nineteenth birthday, which was why he had decided to shoot the rapids, proving no one, not even this young Marine with his Colorado machismo, was invincible. I was thinking about the dead Marine's family, imagining some sort of mundane task his mother would be doing—making the bed or sorting laundry—at the very moment she would receive the news, when Corporal Gomez sidled up and attempted a second introduction with such cheerfulness I was compelled to gaze back at the dead Marine's face.

Later, Gomez brought a lantern for my tent. Outside, the air was mountain fresh and cool. Inside, the air was dry and dusty. I wanted to tie open the tent flap, encourage a breeze, but Gomez had warned about raccoons.

I unrolled my sleeping bag, and after changing into running shorts and one of Tom's T-shirts, I felt the first rush of hot liquid between my legs. I stripped off the shorts and grabbed a hand towel from the truck. Blood was dripping down my legs faster than I could wipe, and quickly soaking through the towel; there was blood on my hands and blood on the floor of the tent. I grabbed another towel, stuffed it between my legs, and redressed. After wiping up the tent floor, I scrambled fifty yards or so for an old, white concrete building that housed the head. The boisterous laughter of young men emanated from inside. I leaned against the outer wall and waited. One by one they exited the head with their towels, plastic soap dishes, and toothbrushes. The last one gestured a thumbs up signal, and I hurried in and showered.

By morning, I had bled through a half dozen tampons I'd at least had the foresight to pack. I thought of Tom back at Camp Pendleton, oblivious to my situation. I had been determined not to tell him, certainly could not leave him a note: *Miscarried last night. See you in a few days. Love you!* Before I was halfway to Bridgeport, I had falsely convinced myself the home pregnancy test had been inaccurate, that I hadn't been pregnant at all, that the heavy bleeding was most likely from the onset of an overdue period. I was delusional, of course. I was hemorrhaging with three days of mountain warfare training ahead of me, unless I exposed the dilemma to the battalion commander.

When I emerged from the tent the next morning, Gomez was just turning off the jeep engine. "You look a little pale this morning, Sergeant," he said, walking around the front of the jeep to open the passenger door. "Sleep okay?"

"In this mountain air? You bet," I said, and jumped in.

At the mess tent, I forced down the watery eggs and limp bacon. We saved the cartons of milk for the jeep ride to the river, where Marine instructors, he told me, would be giving instructions on how to ford streams the way I'd seen the others do the night before to retrieve the drowned Marine. In the jeep, Gomez followed snakelike curves around rocky ridges etched out by the river below, and the drive reminded me of the one Tom and I had taken up the Pacific Coast Highway a few months earlier.

"Rocks!" Gomez shouted, and swerved to avoid the rumbling slide of shale and debris from the cliff on my side of the road. "You have to watch for falling rocks," he said too loud, almost boastful. "They'll kill us in this open jeep."

By the time we arrived, Marines were already in the river, four at a time, arm in arm, moving forward on commands to *Step . . . step . . . step . . .* I shot a roll of film before realizing the best photos would come from the other side, where I could capture facial expressions. But to get to the other side, I had to cross the river: I volunteered for the next group. After draping the cameras around my neck, I locked arms at the elbows of the men to my left and right, and on the command to step, leading with the left foot, we entered the cold river.

The trick to fording a stream is to remain visibly focused on the shore ahead and not on the water that is swirling around your legs. Similar to the advice one might give about not looking down to someone with a fear of heights. My group was moving in sync, pausing long enough for each to gain balance against a rocky, stirring river bottom before taking the next step. If my partners were being extra cautious because they had a woman with them, I was unaware.

Halfway across the river when we were now hip deep in it, a flood of warm blood spilled into my pants. I focused on the shoreline, resisting the urge to reassure myself the river wasn't running red between my legs.

Once ashore, I gave thanks for the camouflage of a wet uniform. I coolly snapped a few photos, and then climbed up a steep, rocky trail that led to the road where Gomez was waiting, leaning against the door of the jeep, a twig in his mouth.

"I want to change into a dry uniform," I blurted.

Gomez pulled the twig from his mouth and tossed it away. "Aye-aye, Sergeant." He scrambled to open the door, but too late. I was already ahead of him.

Back at the tent, my hands were shaking, which made pulling off the heavy wet clothing and boots even more difficult. But once I was in dry clothes, I felt a sense of comfort. I was, however, growing anxious about my depleting tampon supply. After all, there were no stores in a mountain wilderness, or access to another woman's supply. Before leaving the tent, I stuffed a hand towel between my legs for insurance.

Gomez had not lied when he said he knew the best spots for photographs. Day two, he'd veered onto a rocky trail and halted the jeep before a jaw-dropping vista. We sat atop a boulder to eat lunch, our legs dangling over the edge of a cliff. Afterward, we'd driven to a site where Marines were learning to scale the smooth rock face of a three-hundred-foot cliff.

"You should try it," Gomez said. He was leaning against the jeep, another twig dangling from his mouth.

"I don't think so." I popped a new canister of film into my camera. Rappelling meant succumbing to a physical security check of ropes between my legs by the rappel master—something, given my current state, I wanted to avoid.

"It will add experience to your story."

"Not today," I said. "I need to stay focused on the job . . . getting photos of these Marines is more important."

When I finished snapping photographs and recording interviews, I walked back to the jeep. Gomez was still leaning against it, and his raised brows hinted at a question. "Don't take this wrong, Sergeant," he said, and had now moved to my side of the jeep, "but you don't look so good. You're white as a ghost."

"Really?" I hopped in. "I feel great. Where next?"

Gomez closed my door and walked around the front of the jeep, throwing suspicious glances at me all the way. My hands were shaking, fumbling through the motions of replacing the spent film cartridge with a new one. Gomez slid behind the wheel, leaned over, and put his hand, warm as a hot brick, on mine. "You're sick, Ma'am," he said. "We need to get you to a doctor."

"Corporal, I'm fine." I slid my hand from his. "Now let's go."

Reluctantly, he cranked the jeep's engine and shifted into first. "Altitude sickness kills people, you know."

If only my problem had been as simple as altitude sickness. Altitude sickness held no gender preference, and would at least create a more respectable way of falling out in front of all these men. How many times had I been accused of martyrdom for the sake of advancing women? My husband and my mother had warned about pushing my body too far with too many five-mile runs, placing myself in too many risky situations. I had made it a habit of dismissing warnings.

We sped off to catch up with Marines marching in a single file on a short hump as acclimation training for the next day's climb to ten thousand feet. I asked Gomez to halt the jeep, and I jumped out, running ahead of the walking column to capture photo opportunities, and then I ran back to the jeep, mostly to prove something to Gomez.

He was quiet on the drive back to the base camp, too. In fact, he did not speak at all until he parked in front of my tent. "You don't have to make that hump up the mountain tomorrow, Ma'am. I can drive you. You can take photos at all the best spots from the jeep."

"Admit it, Gomez," I teased, climbing out of the jeep, "you just want an easy ride to the top. When I leave here in a few days, you're going to have to get a real job."

"I have my hands full with you right now."

The next morning at chow Gomez sidled up to me with a tray of food. "Still hard-headed on humping up the mountain?"

"Still looking for an excuse not to?" The food on his tray made me want to puke. I grabbed my juice and apple and headed to one of the empty tables.

"I've got an idea," I heard from behind. Gomez was following me. He set his tray down and climbed over the picnic table bench. "Why don't you hump up and ride back?

"And then you won't have to hump at all, right?" I needed distance from the smell of his breakfast. This time when I stood up, Gomez grabbed the bottom edge of my cammie jacket, and held firm.

"You don't have to prove anything to anybody, Ma'am. You're from Public Affairs, not Seventh Marines. Just do your job—"

I leaned over. "I *am* doing my job, Corporal Gomez. Why don't you do yours?

"Your hands are still shaking, and you look like *shit!*"

I fought the instinct to storm off, and sat back down. "Look, I'll hump up and ride back. Satisfied?" Truth was, I was relieved.

Head down and move out, keep your eyes on the man in front of you, change your socks every three to four miles, don't think just walk, and when you think you can't walk another step, walk another, and another, and another, and . . .

During the climb, I was now struggling for each breath. The others broke into exuberant singing cadence: *Mama and Papa were lying in bed . . .* But all I could muster were a few whispered attempts. *Mama rolled over and this is what she said . . .* The June morning, once cool, even more so in the stretches of road flanked by the evergreens, was swelling into a thick haze. Sweat dripped into my boots—at least I hoped it was sweat—and the bottoms of my feet were stinging as if I were walking barefoot over rough, hot asphalt. The blood-soaked towel between my legs was gaining weight, and heat, in my trousers. What I wouldn't give to be like the man in front of me, so seemingly comfortable in his own skin. How much farther could I go like this? The voice in my head answered, *As far as anyone else.*

We stopped long enough to change socks and to lunch on MREs. I wasn't interested in lunch. I strolled as far as I could from the men who were swapping meals and comparing blisters, and eased myself to the ground under a copse of tall evergreens. When I leaned over to pull off my left boot, I peeked between my legs. So far, so good.

With shaky fingers, I applied bandages to my blisters, and then settled back onto a bed of thick pine needles. A cool breeze blew across my bare, bandaged feet, and I shivered. In fact, the stability of the ground beneath me made me even more aware of my body's shakiness. I was feverish and in serious trouble. If only Gomez would show up now . . .

I stared into the top branches of the trees, eager to find the sun, but the swaying branches were uncooperative, providing instead, a dizzying kaleidoscope of green and gold.

An hour or so later, I was catching my breath at ten thousand feet on a mountain top sparsely covered in ice. The Marines who had beaten me to the top were already sprawled with outstretched limbs along thin patches of green or were shirtless and bootless, sunning themselves like lizards across boulders. Others were either eating MREs or changing socks and bitching about the climb down as they held up raw-pink bare feet to compare blisters. I climbed atop a warm boulder, but with the extra exertion came another hot spill of blood. Turning my back on everyone, and while unlacing and pulling off my boots, I checked for signs of blood between my legs. A thin, dark-red patch high enough in the crotch to remain undetectable raised my spirits. I whisked off my socks, nonchalantly made note of the two new blisters on my left foot and the one on my right heel, and was applying fresh bandages when I heard someone's boots crunching in the ice behind me.

Gomez was smiling. "Looking for a ride?"

I shrugged and turned sideways to ensure Gomez could not see my soiled pants as I pulled on fresh socks and laced up my boots. When I was finished, he extended a hand to help me from the boulder. "You did great," he added. "They're all talking about how you hung in there and kept up."

"Now they'll be saying something else," I said, "when they see me ride past them in a jeep." And for once, I did not care.

That evening, Gomez tossed my gear into a van that was to return me and a handful of other Marines back to Camp Pendleton.

"Thanks for everything," I said, and extended a hand.

"I hope you get to feeling better."

I rolled my eyes and climbed into the van, settling onto the third seat from the front, scooting to the window, and mouthed to Gomez, *I'm fine.* Now it was his turn to roll his eyes.

Two hours into the return trip home, we stopped at a diner. I had not eaten since the apple at breakfast, but the assault of onions and grease was too much. I excused myself, and was climbing back into the van to wait when a sudden sharpness in my lower left abdomen, as if something were burning a hole to get out, caused me to double over. I sank across the first bench seat, and lay curled up with pain.

Some time later, the van rocked under the weight of each returning Marine.

"Hey, Sergeant," I heard, "you okay?"

I could not answer.

Then I heard, "She's passing out!"

And, "Where's a hospital?"

"I don't know, man, run back in and ask somebody."

"How long have you been hemorrhaging?" a nurse asked. I was at Edwards Air Force Base, which is where, ironically, I'd been a little more than a year earlier to photograph the landing of the *Columbia* shuttle—and where on the same lake-bed runway Sally Ride's *Challenger* was scheduled to land, God willing.

Standing in the doorway were the Marines from the van, their faces anxious and uncomfortable. "About four days," I told the nurse. The Marines stole glances at one another and then settled their stares on the floor.

Another nurse walked in the room and to the telephone on the wall. She punched a blinking line. "It's for you, your office at Public Affairs."

All Top Hunter had to say was, "Hey, what happened?" and I burst into tears. Something in the somber familiarity of his tone confirmed the danger I was in. The Marines leaning against the wall across the room shifted their stances while I blubbered into the phone, "I'm not sure, Top, but the story and film are in my deuce gear."

"For Christ's sake, I don't care about that. Are you okay?"

"You don't care?" I said, but my brain was screaming, *How could you not fucking care?* "Look," I added, and to the worried faces hanging around the door, "these Marines are going to promise to go on to Pendleton tonight. They're going to promise to deliver my gear to Public Affairs. The film and story will be in there."

The Marines reverently mumbled good-byes as the nurse pulled a curtain around me.

An ectopic pregnancy is one in which a fertilized egg begins to grow outside the uterus, a life-threatening situation, especially if the egg begins to grow within a fallopian tube. Symptoms are severe pain, nausea, bleeding, and the sudden loss of tissue . . . The egg will eventually rupture the fallopian tube, causing severe hemorrhaging. Infertility may result when infection affects the uterus and the secondary fallopian tube.

When I awakened from surgery, I found Tom folded in the chair beside the bed. Across his forehead, lines were now permanently etched so that even in sleep he appeared worried. His hands lay casually across both thighs.

I was still watching him restlessly sleep when the surgeon entered, causing Tom to jump to his feet and to my bedside.

"You must have been in excruciating pain for days," the surgeon said.

"Not until last night."

"That's impossible." He glanced toward Tom. "That's what I call the power of the mind over the body."

The damaged portion of my left fallopian tube had been removed. The operation had also revealed unrelated damage to my right tube that meant it was impossible for me to ever have another child. My martyrdom had stopped short of killing me, but it had robbed me of my fertility. After the surgeon left us alone, I stared at the hospital room ceiling, the doctor's words still resonating in my brain as if he were still standing beside the bed, repeating himself over and over . . . *You're infertile, infertile.* Tom, unmistakably glum, had left the room on a pretense for coffee.

I was suddenly aware of how much I had taken for granted. Since joining the Marines I had fought to defeat every clue of my body's femaleness as well as what I and the men around me perceived as female weakness. What had happened to the little girl who once daydreamed of her body developing into her mother's movie-star shape?

I was eight before noticing my mother was a figure with breasts. She had taken me along to one of her dog obedience classes. Leaning against the brick wall of a shopping center and watching her maneuver one of our pets among fellow trainers and their dogs, I swelled with love for my mother in that moment, loving her for being more beautiful than any other mother I knew.

She was wearing a putty-colored mock turtleneck that day. I remember it clearly: the turtleneck molded with the shape of her breasts. A chocolate tweed skirt with a running thread of royal blue draped her hips and fell modestly to the middle of her knees, knees that were a model for my own. Her figure, neat and trim with shoulders the same width as her hips, had reminded me of my grandmother's hourglass that I used to play with when I couldn't sleep during naptimes.

Later that night, when my mother came to my bedside to hear my prayers, I had lifted my pajama top and scooped as much eight-year-old breast tissue as I could from under my arms to the breastbone and declared, "Look Mom, I need a bra like you."

Years of flattening my breasts with too-small bras and squeezing into too-tight girdles in an effort to hide the female in this male world had defeated my body. It was Darwinian, of course. Why study finches and their beak adaptations when I was living proof of Darwin's theory of evolution? Proof of natural selection? I was the female trying to survive in a male-dominated society whose body was progressively becoming more male-like, starting with the elimination of its entire reproductive capabilities. Any day now I supposed I could look forward to the sprouting of hair on my chest and upper lip.

However, my mind was wrestling with another theory that day in the hospital room, a theory that had been generated from the last memory I have of my maternal grandmother before she died from breast cancer.

It had been a morning when I was about twelve. My grandmother's farmhouse kitchen was filling with the aroma of field peas we had picked before breakfast. I was drying the breakfast dishes as my grandmother washed and rinsed them. She was telling me a story about how she used to play the organ and sing on the radio in the thirties, in those years before she married my grandfather and he'd made her stop, though he allowed her to play the organ every Christmas for the grandchildren who gathered around her to sing carols. Above her organ hung my favorite photograph of her as a young woman dressed in a long, ruffled white gown, seated with straight-back royalty at a piano for what looked to be a formal affair.

So on this morning in her kitchen, as I was drying the last dish, I asked her why she never sang anymore.

"Can't," she said, taking the dish from my hand and setting it onto the shelf. "God takes away the gifts you refuse."

★

For the next two years, I immersed myself in work as the beat reporter for both the Fifth and Seventh Marine Regiments, as well as for Marine Aircraft Group 39. When John Lehman, then secretary of the Navy on a tour of Camp Pendleton, crawled into the cockpit of a Huey helicopter to clock a few hours of his Reserve time, I was there, snapping photographs. Afterward, as he walked toward an idling sedan near the tarmac for the ride to a field position where a battalion of infantrymen awaited his arrival, he invited me to ride along in his staff car rather than follow behind in the wake of security and press vehicles, and this had given me an opportunity to draw him out about his love and admiration for the Marines. On his leather jacket, he had replaced the Velcro name patch of "John A. Lehman, Secretary of the Navy" with "John A. Lehman, *Secretary of the Marine Corps*," for which there is no such position.

Shortly after my interview with Lehman, I ran into Col. John Hopkins. It was during a reception for the commandant, General Barrow, who was aboard the base for a final tour before retirement to Louisiana. Tom and I hated attending these functions. There are two worlds in the military: officer and enlisted. In those days, the clubs were marked officer and enlisted; the heads were marked officer and enlisted; at one time, even the water fountains. When we attended a function at the officers' club, Tom and I felt awkward, stared at, as reproached as any interracial couple in those days. Tom was a captain by then and obligated to attend. As his wife, I was obligated as well.

At these formal affairs, Tom and other officers wore dress uniforms; I wore civilian clothing and tried to blend in with the other wives, although that wasn't always so easy to do. On the night of Barrow's reception, the commandant recognized me as the Public Affairs journalist who had followed him around all day with a camera and a huge telephoto lens. My assignment for the base newspaper had been to cover the commandant's last official visit. At one point during the day, when Barrow was walking with several other officers toward the reviewing stand for the First Marine Division military parade—each man instinctively keeping time to the band's spirited rendition of "Semper Fidelis"—Barrow suddenly fell out of step, changed directions, and headed in mine. As he drew closer, I jumped to attention and saluted, letting the heavy camera with its long telephoto lens dangle from its strap around my neck.

"Sergeant," said General Barrow in his gentle Louisiana drawl, "give me that camera."

"Yes, Sir." I ended the salute, lifted the camera from around my neck, and handed it over.

Barrow called out, "Sergeant Major! Come here, please."

Sergeant Major Crawford, the sergeant major of the Marine Corps, had been talking with a small circle of young enlisted Marines. He shook the hand of one Marine and slapped the back of another before heading in our direction. He was smiling as he approached us.

"Sergeant Major, I want you to take a picture of this young lady with me. She's been following me all day with this heavy thing. Someone needs to be taking *her* picture."

The general placed an arm around my shoulder and the sergeant major said, "Say Ooorah!" before snapping the photo.

That evening, at Barrow's reception, I was standing next to Tom when my eyes met General Barrow's. He was in dress blues, as all the officers were, men and women, and was in a discussion with Major General Day, the division commanding general. A minute or so later, I felt Tom's body beside me stiffen.

"Good evening, Sir."

I turned to see the commandant shaking hands with my husband.

"Good evening, Captain," in that long drawl of General Barrow's. "I don't believe we've met, although I've had the pleasure of meeting this young lady."

Tom looked too stunned for words: half in awe, half in fright he had been exposed for bringing a sergeant to the commandant's reception.

I stepped forward and put my hand out. "Good evening, Sir. With your permission, may I present my husband." It was then, just beyond the commandant's left shoulder, that I caught a glimpse of Col. John Hopkins for the first time since that day on the mountain at Twentynine Palms. Now, instead of cammies and boots, he was dressed in full uniform regalia that included the Silver Star. On his face, a wide smile for me that suggested we shared a secret.

★

My name appeared on the staff sergeant promotion list the same year Colonel Hopkins's name appeared on the brigadier general list. I made the presumptuous decision to call his office at Fifth Marines and leave him a congratulatory message, surprised when my call was put through immediately to him.

"And did I hear," said Hopkins, "that you've submitted a package for warrant officer?" How had he known this?

"Yes, Sir."

"It's a tough selection process . . . some have to reapply three or more times."

"Yes, Sir, that's what I hear, Colonel."

There had been an awkward pause, and then, "You'll make a fine officer, Tracy." There, my first name. One of the few times I had heard it spoken since joining the Marines six years earlier. I suspected the colonel's use of my first name was an attempt to convey what military rules and regulations were enacted to prevent.

A few months later, Tom received orders to Yorktown Naval Weapons Station in Virginia. This was 1984, the beginning of Reagan's second term. For my birthday, which happens to fall on Inauguration Day every four years, Tom surprised me with tickets to the Young Americans Ball.

I'd managed to snag a position at the Little Creek Naval Amphibious Base in Norfolk, an hour south of Yorktown, although this involved a drive through the underwater Hampton Roads Bridge Tunnel each day. I was assigned to work for Brig. Gen. Carl Mundy, who later also became commandant. And, Hopkins, a brigadier general, was assigned to the Marine Expeditionary Force at Camp Lejeune, North Carolina, five hours south of Norfolk.

It seems now as I think back to it that the warrant officer selection list had been delayed for some reason. General Mundy, in an effort to ease impending disappointment, had called me into his office one afternoon. "How would you like to go to Norway in a few months for the NATO exercise?" I thanked him for the opportunity, and as I moved to begin an about-face, he added, "You know, a promotion to bird colonel is easier to get than a promotion to warrant officer."

But a few days later, on a late Friday afternoon, Tom was standing in the middle of the daycare parking lot, waving his arms. I was feeling frazzled from having been held up, or under, if you will, in the Hampton Roads Bridge Tunnel because of someone's fender bender.

I parked, and Tom yanked open the car door, pulled me into the parking lot, and swung me into the air. "You did it!"

"Did what?"

"You made warrant officer!"

When he set me down onto the gravel parking lot, I saw Morgan with her face pressed against the window of her classroom. She was all eyes and mouth. I felt a rush of shame. In a few weeks, thanks to the promotion, I would have to leave her again, and this time for nearly three months of officer training at Quantico.

★

After chow one evening at Quantico, I climbed to the windy top of the metal bleachers with the others from my platoon. We wiggled along the cold seats until everyone was shoulder to shoulder and hip to hip, allowing room for the four platoons now marching from the chow hall with a thumping boot cadence that made the metal beneath me hum. This was April 1985. The time of the night compass march. The true test, some had said, of courage and leadership.

I was one of nine women squeezed in among the tall bodies of men who in their bulky field jackets and cammies made staying warm that chilly evening in northern Virginia nearly possible.

When all five platoons had scooted into tight sitting formations, our training officer hopped onto the bottom bleacher. "Look up," he said, pointing toward the lilac phase of sunset. "You'll notice there's no moon tonight, unlike last week's practice session." I was envisioning the ancient mariners on a night such as this; salty sea captains at the helms of long wooden boats, helplessly adrift on swells during nights when the moon and the constellations were as out of sight as land in the middle of the sea. What would they have given for our compasses, our knowledge about navigation?

The training officer explained that at nightfall we would travel about a mile if we stayed on course, two or more if we got lost. The goal, he added, was to navigate unfamiliar terrain to a row of metal ammo boxes we would find spaced fifty feet apart. To pass, we would have to land precisely at the correct ammo box for our coordinates. He warned about the river, how it was overflowing because of the beaver dams, and *Don't fall into a beaver dam!* I pinpointed the river on my map. Drew a black circle around the exact crossing.

Lessons learned in training save lives during combat! Last to know, first to go! A Marine officer has to know how to read a map, how to plot coordinates for artillery fire that won't wipe out friendlies. A Marine officer has to know how to lead Marines into and out of combat zones because, as everyone knows, one wrong turn could get everyone killed.

Admittedly, our combat training in Quantico was during the middle of a relatively quiet era in military history if you discounted the invasion into Grenada, Cold War threats, a bombing raid on Tripoli, and the peacekeeping mission in Beirut that had turned anything but peaceful. War with the Soviets still felt imminent, and our fear of war, along with a healthy fear of failure, compelled us to take seriously each training exercise, even if conditions at Quantico were artificially manufactured.

A week earlier, during the practice for this final night compass march, and sitting on these same bleachers, each of us had drawn coordinates and then shot azimuths, plotting them on our maps with protractors and compasses. We were marched under a full moon to a wooded area. The signal, a pistol crack, had set us off on foot through a hundred yards of forest that seemingly conspired against us by pulling a shade to the moonlight.

I tripped over roots, lost count of my steps, and had to backtrack. I offered my hand in an outstretched sacrifice to the wicked vines and low hanging limbs that otherwise slashed at my face and neck. I feared for my eyes mostly, fighting the imaginary sharp sticks as they darted toward me. And then there had been the crackle of limbs and leaves, a holler from someone who tripped, a nervous giggle, and the "OORAH!" from the first Marine who made it through to smooth asphalt. When I stumbled from the darkness to an umbrella of light beneath a streetlamp, I found myself at the feet of a smiling lance corporal who verified my success by writing on my card a fat black checkmark.

The training officer paced the length of the metal bleachers, waiting for the lists of coordinates to make their way among 230. When I had mine, I quickly plotted my coordinates, balancing compass and pen and map protractor on my lap. I should admit to feeling overly confident. Not only had I passed the practice march, but I had remained behind at Quantico the weekend before, Easter weekend, with Himes, Johnson, and a handful of others for additional training.

Although there had been other separations during our marriage, Tom's ability to cope as a single parent had reduced with each, and after eight weeks in Quantico, I was fully questioning my decision to become an officer. "Not coming home for Easter?" he said the night I called. I leaned against the wall in the barrack's lounge, winding and rewinding the telephone cord around my index finger. "But that's two weekends in a row."

"This Monday," I'd explained, "is the night compass march. I need to practice this weekend."

"But it's Easter," Tom said. "What am I supposed to tell our daughter?"

I gave the phone cord one long tug, a long sigh. "I know, I know, but she's only four and a half."

Geographically, Quantico was two hours north from our home in Hampton, and I felt fortunate to have made it home several weekends. Three other women who were also mothers didn't live close enough to commute; they spent their weekends in uninterrupted blocks of study time for tests on Soviet weapon systems and on nuclear, biological, and chemical warfare. And then there had been the outburst of chicken pox—Tom hadn't known you shouldn't place a child with chicken pox in a tub of water. After six years of marriage, I was learning he didn't know a great deal about anything outside his military self, which these days, close to retirement, included golf handicaps more than General Orders.

But at night in my room at the barracks, I lay in a single bunk with my M-16 rifle locked to the bed frame, and pictured Tom a hundred miles away in our bed, our daughter in hers, tucked beneath a Sleeping Beauty bedspread. One day I would have to answer for all this, for leaving them for months at a time. Too, I wondered what our daughter would think about having been raised by two parents who had been trained to kill.

I'd had a revelation about Tom a few weeks earlier during another night exercise. It was the night all five platoons were driven to a live-firing range at dusk, where we were divided into groups of two and instructed to dig fighting holes. The winter ground had been cold and unyielding. I had struggled to match my partner, a man, shovel for shovel, and despite the cold air that felt closer to winter than spring, I was perspiring. My feet, however, felt numb and my fingers, like brittle sticks, ready to snap.

After digging to four feet, we propped our machine guns on the upper edge of the bunker, positioning the weapons into what would be intersecting fields of fire. When the shrill whistle alerted us to commence firing, I lunged for the machine gun and squeezed off rounds, hot cartridge shells grazing my hands and cheeks. My jolting body became one with machine; my mind, however, floated with the red sea of tracer bullets crisscrossing with such precision, such danger, such beauty I hated to see it all diminished by the white flares shot into the black holes of space to illuminate a make-believe enemy. This, I thought, is what combat looks like. Beautiful, just before the ugliness. And, if we were lucky, this would be the closest to combat we would ever get. This, I remember thinking, too, was what Tom must have seen in Vietnam, and now I was seeing him not as the combat officer he had become, but as the frightened private he must have been in '68, in Da Nang and Hue. How had he, how had anyone faced this red scissoring—of friendly fire intersected with enemy? And I suddenly understood why, in the commissary on Okinawa several years earlier, as I had been pushing our infant daughter in the stroller behind him down the aisle of canned meats and vegetables and past an old woman with bright eyes who was speaking Vietnamese to her daughter, Tom had dropped the can of tuna and flattened himself against the shelves.

Back in the barrack's lounge, though, among the rows of black-and-silver telephones, I heard Tom say he wanted me home for Easter. Another woman Marine from my platoon shuffled into the lounge. She smiled, headed for a telephone across the room, and inserted a fistful of quarters that were clinking as if falling from a slot machine.

I turned my back on her and wound the telephone cord around my finger. "Three weeks," I whispered into the phone. "You can hang on that long, can't you?" In three weeks, I would pack the new uniforms—the dress blues and the dress whites—the ivory-handled officer's sword, the weapons guidebooks on machine guns, howitzers, and Soviet tanks, and put Quantico in the rear-view mirror. And once home? Then what? All that awkwardness of trying to become again the wife and mother I had been forced to let go of for so many weeks. What if I couldn't become all that again? Three weeks: twenty-one days. Hadn't I read somewhere it took just twenty-one days to establish a habit? Or, had that been to break one? "I really need to stay for this extra navigation training."

"You're becoming impossible!" he shouted.

I gave the phone cord a final tug. "Didn't you fail the night compass march?"

At 2:00 a.m. Easter Sunday, the day before the final night compass march, I heard a knock. From my bunk to the door, I dragged the dream of the day's navigation practice over brown hills—the smell of cold, lifeless trees still in my hair—and the memory of counting and recounting my steps, of refiguring grid north from geographic north from magnetic north in an effort to find true north. I opened the door and Tom was there, in his arms our sleeping toddler with a blush of the pox on her chin, shoeless, lost in her own dreams, wearing the new Easter dress. Rumpled.

For the night compass march, you set off on foot at nightfall, and at first everything seems almost pleasant. You're bundled in a heavy field jacket over your cammies, you're wearing boots, and around your waist you have a belt with a canteen of water. You have a flashlight and a compass with a red needle that points toward magnetic north regardless of the direction you turn your body. The trick is in remembering to turn your body and compass as one.

Forty, forty-one, forty-two . . . sixty-five steps per hundred meters, and you're mentally tracking the meters and the steps across dark dry acres and up and over small hills. You could get used to this, this thrill of independence that is feeding your spirit, of self-reliance; for the first time you know where you are and where you need to go.

After a while, you start wondering how everyone else is getting along. You shine the flashlight on your wristwatch; nearly an hour has passed since you last heard another Marine . . . and now you are beginning to slow down. You fix in your mind the step count, so you can stop, have a look around without losing your place. You check left and listen. Nothing. No crickets, no frogs, no birds. You check right. Nothing but the noise in your head and the roar of silence in your ears. You think, *What are the odds I'm the only one in more than two hundred to have drawn these coordinates?* And then it happens. That sliding silver pinball that rolls and rolls around in your brain until it drops like cold metal into your heart: you're lost. Or maybe, just maybe, you're the only one on the true trail. That's it, you say. You're right, for after all, hadn't you made it through the dark forest last week? In the classroom, hadn't you correctly plotted every coordinate? You refer to your map for the elevation, searching on paper for the depression you're standing in. You walk on. Up and over another hill toward the sound of rapids. The river. And so you must be right.

The icy water swirls around your ankles and you trudge on up to the knees, to the hips, to the waist, holding your ground, stopping to check your compass, remembering when you learned to cross a river two years earlier at mountain warfare training in northern California how easy it is to be swept away or pulled off course, and so you adjust, lift a foot, place it down, slide another along the unsettled bottom until the river around you sinks from your waist to hips, to knees, to ankles. Downstream, the crash of limbs: *Goddam beavers!* you hear from someone downstream. You shout into the cavern of darkness toward the voice, *Everything okay?* A reluctant, *Yeah!* sends you back on course.

A half hour later, your toes are stubbing against asphalt. Something's wrong here, you think, and you pull out the map, click on the flashlight. Look up. You've learned true north can be found by locating the moon and its angle to the North Star. But there's no moon, remember? But neither is there supposed to be a road here under your feet. What you want to think is, *Who put this goddam road here?* What you're really thinking is, *Who forgot to put this road on the goddam map?* Because what you don't want to think is, *How the hell did I wander so far off course I found a road not on the goddam map?* And you're wondering if you're even on the fucking base anymore. And where the hell is everybody? And how long will they wait before sending out a search party? And how if you'd been able to eat more for dinner than a package of peanut butter crackers—only a sadist orders a weigh-in after chow—you would be thinking more clearly. And you've decided that when you get back to the barracks, if you get back, you're going to order a large pepperoni pizza with double cheese from that place that delivers on base until midnight. Then you stomp the road and curse at the sky because there's no one here to act shocked and because yelling is the one thing you can control right now and because the sound of your voice feels a little less lonely. And you cry, because no one's here to see.

You read somewhere that scientists believe the magnetic poles reverse themselves every five hundred thousand years or so—meaning what is north today flips south tomorrow—and since Earth is apparently long overdue for a reversal of magnetic poles . . . suppose your compass needle has been pointing south all along? You picture your husband, smug when you tell him you failed the night compass march after ruining the family's Easter weekend, and this makes you wish the poles had reversed themselves, that if you have to fail the night compass march, then let your failure come as a result of a cataclysmic event. And then you stuff the map and compass into your field jacket pocket, make a half turn toward the direction from where you came, and walk on, just walking, no longer thinking or caring about step counts and meters, for what does all that matter if your whole world has turned upside down.

The next time your feet touch asphalt they're near an ammo box. Squint hard and you can just make out the line of the other ammo boxes along the shoulder of the road. Marines are emerging ghostlike, one and two at a time from the trees, halting by their boxes, silently handing over their cards to enlisted Marines. You're waiting for the lance corporal at yours as he compares your coordinates with the number on the ammo box. He looks into your face. "Ma'am," he says, "you landed at the very opposite end of the course."

You extend a shaky hand for the card. "Damn beavers," you say, but you're thinking, *So this is failure* . . . This is what your husband felt that night seven years ago when he failed the night compass march, and you're wishing for a way to make it up to him.

The lance corporal leans over you, whispers, "Get back into the woods, Ma'am . . . walk all the way down to the last box." And then he's shoving you out of sight. At first, your feet refuse to budge, but that's okay because your mind has already raced on without them: a hundred flashes of the past, present, and future hanging on your next decision. A true test of courage and leadership.

Then you're zigzagging through the forest, welcoming the thorny vines that slash your face and neck. You're falling over stumps and limbs, and picking yourself up, and ignoring the pain in your knee and the swelling of your ankle. Your left cheek stings and you wonder if the scar will be permanent.

You come out the other end of the dark forest, changed. You won't go to the last box; you take the one second from the end. A perfect score you can't stomach. You'll give your husband that satisfaction. Another lance corporal takes your card, jots down the number, and says, "Congratulations, Ma'am, you have successfully navigated the night compass march."

You mutter a thanks and secretly vow to practice every weekend until you can plot true north with your eyes closed. As you shuffle toward the cattle car up ahead that's idling on the shoulder of the road, you're thinking, *Sure, this may be peacetime, but how long could anyone expect it to last?* You spot Himes, who is now boarding the cattle car. You grab the bottom edge of his field jacket. Yank him from the steps. He smells of woods and dirt and sweat. On his neck, a nasty scratch resembles a thread of beaded garnets.

"I went to the wrong box . . ."

"Shhh!" he says, grabbing a fistful of your jacket to pull you closer. "Everybody did . . ."

THREE

★

After Quantico, I'm assigned as the Public Affairs officer to the New River Air Station in Jacksonville, North Carolina. This time, Tom follows *me*. He is assigned to nearby Camp Lejeune.

We're renting a spacious four-bedroom Victorian down the street from our closest friends. Tom and I host poker parties and Sunday football gatherings. Most Friday nights, we meet friends at a club in Jacksonville for hours and hours of dancing. We buy a fifteen-foot boat from Himes, and spend summer weekends, when Tom's not playing golf, skiing up and down the intracoastal waterway. Morgan is in kindergarten and learning to ride a bike. Like most young couples, Tom and I are feeling the pressures of spending more than we make, thanks in some part to Tom's gambling habits on the golf course. When I am sent for three months to the University of Oklahoma for military-sponsored courses in mass communications, I learn to thrive under the freedom of being single. I return full of myself, and ask Tom for a divorce, a separation that only lasts three months. Soon, we are back to our life of poker parties and expensive golf outings.

A few months after our reconciliation, from a radio somewhere in the New River Public Affairs office, Tina Turner is belting "What's Love Got to Do with It" as the telephone in my office rings.

"Public Affairs, Warrant Officer . . ."

It's 1987, just four days from the day I will be fired, but of course, I don't know this yet. In a chair on the other side of my desk, Sgt. Marie Flowers is hunched over a stack of dummy layouts and possible photographs for the front page of our base newspaper.

When I set the phone into the cradle, she narrows her eyes into slits.

"It was him, wasn't it?"

I shrug and glance down at the stack of layouts.

"That crazy bastard!"

She flings herself into the back of her chair and the chair smacks against the wall.

"Careful, you're talking about our CO."

Flowers, in that nervous habit of hers, begins pulling eyelashes from the rims of her dark exotic eyes. "What about Headquarters Marine Corps?"

I shake my head.

"Boomer?"

"I doubt General Boomer even knows our CO."

Besides, I hadn't been the only officer on the CO's staff to receive threatening phone calls. What he said to the others, though, I couldn't tell you. What he said to me was always the same: *I'm watching you. I know what you're doing.* A month earlier, his admin officer, a likeable captain with a ready smile, had broken under the CO's pressure and had attempted suicide. The captain was still locked away in the psych ward at the hospital on Lejeune.

"What we need to do," I say to Flowers, who appears in a trance as she plucks eyelashes, "is hop a Huey."

She stops plucking. "For what?"

"There's that story we need to cover about SPIE rigging. Why don't we do it together, rather than put this one on Sergeant Tripp? He's overloaded as it is."

By then, I had already decided it had been a mistake to become an officer. The best rank in the Marine Corps is sergeant. As a sergeant, you're a leader and yet malleable enough to be influenced and shaped by the officers around you, especially by officers who, like me, remember what it's like to be a sergeant. That's why so many regular officers disliked warrant officers. With no enlisted experience, a regular officer wasn't likely to garner the level of respect a warrant officer would.

I had wanted my sergeants to encounter the same richness of experience I had as a sergeant. I wanted them to cover the stories that would win journalism and photography awards as I had won. I wanted to see them hone skills and leadership abilities that would prepare them to become either staff noncommissioned officers or warrant officers, if they chose. As their Public Affairs officer, I sought opportunities for them. I sent Flowers to New York City one Fourth of July weekend by helicopter to snap a photograph of President Reagan on an aircraft carrier. Her stunning photography of a helicopter on a flyby of the Statue of Liberty was published by a number of military and civilian newspapers. Her photographs of the president and first lady, poignant.

And then there were the stories and photographs captured by Sergeant Tripp and his wife, also a sergeant. When news about events on the air station needed release to the public, I urged Tripp to call out the release to the wire services and local media. He was the one now who needed the experience of being quoted as an official spokesperson. His wife was a gifted writer and a hard worker. I had known them both at Camp Pendleton when I was a sergeant. Now that I was their Public Affairs officer, I felt compelled to provide them, Flowers, and the others with invaluable experiences. So, the next day, Flowers and I, dressed in one-piece flight suits, hopped aboard a Huey from Marine Aircraft Group 26 for the short flight across the New River to Onslow Beach at Lejeune. I let Flowers think her job was to snap photos of SPIE rigging, an acronym for Special Purpose Insertion and Extraction. In short, this is when Marines are harnessed to a thick metal cable, and then hoisted to five hundred feet or so to where they're dangling fifty feet under the helicopter. It's a method for quick insertions and extractions into and out of hot combat zones.

But I hadn't told Flowers everything.

The pilot landed on a sandy pad at the edge of Onslow Beach, and Flowers and I jumped to the ground and ran under the *whomp-whomp* of blades to the platoon of infantrymen who were waiting for a lesson on SPIE rigging. I found the platoon commander, a first lieutenant, and told him Flowers and I wanted the opportunity to SPIE rig as part of our story coverage. Flowers's head jerked above the notepad she'd been using to record names and hometowns.

The lieutenant said he couldn't see a problem; in fact, he said it was likely to calm his men if they saw two women go first . . .

Flowers tugged on the sleeve of my flight suit to pull me aside. "Ma'am, do you know what you're getting us into?"

"Not exactly, but come on, Flowers, you don't want to live your whole life as a Marine in a skirt and high heels, do you?"

"I hadn't thought much about it one way or the other."

A lance corporal and a Pfc. were strapping us into rigging harnesses by weaving straps around our waists, down our legs, and between our upper thighs. A senior enlisted man from the British Royal Marines stood over them, barking orders in an English accent about the importance of safety checks. When the two were finished with their harnessing, they grabbed the cables that had fallen against our crotches, and tugged upward, yanking Flowers and me forward.

"Aye," said the Brit, "you done a bloody good job!" And then,

"If you two *Lidies* will kindly move aside," and as Flowers and I stepped to his left, "now get me two Marine arses over here for riggin'!"

A few minutes later, over the whir of two helicopters, the crew chief was telling the lieutenant, the Brit, and I that the pilots wanted to fly back to New River for refueling. "Just a safety precaution. We'll be back in less than forty." And he turned and ran to one of the helicopters, hunching when he came within blade distance. He hopped onto his backside in the doorway and waved as first his, and then the second bird, lifted off.

Flowers was off to herself, reloading her camera. "Problem," I whispered, "I have to pee."

She looked down at my tied up crotch in the bunched up one-piece flight suit and laughed. "That *is* a problem . . . oh no, now *I* have to go!"

On Onslow Beach, there are cabanas that Marines and their families can rent for the day, and these cabanas with restrooms were within a few hundred yards of the lift point for the SPIE rig exercise. Flowers and I headed to the cabana.

"But how are we going to do this?"

"With these," I said, retrieving two paper cups from a garbage can. "We're going to unzip best we can, stuff a cup between our legs, and pee."

"Standing up? Ma'am . . . I can't . . ."

"Got a better idea?"

"This is working, Ma'am!" Flowers yelled from another stall.

"Sure is." And then I felt warm urine trickle down my right leg. I tried to halt the flow. I maneuvered the cup back out through the opening between flight suit and harness, but the cup became wedged. I pulled too hard and the cup collapsed, spilling its entire contents.

Flowers stared at my crotch. "What happened?"

"I couldn't hold my urine."

We stood on the beach, she facing the platoon of Marines and the landing zone where the helicopters were expected to land any minute while I faced the Atlantic Ocean in hopes the breeze would dry my uniform. "Take another look," I said to Flowers, who then pretended to walk casually toward the water, for the twentieth time in twenty minutes. She turned to walk back, all the while staring at my crotch, and this time she was smiling.

"Now, if we have any mechanical problems up there," the crew chief said as Flowers and I lined up to get snap-linked to a fifty-foot cable, "I'll have to cut." The crew chief, like a mad man, held up a yellow ax as proof he was telling the truth. "And then, you're on your own." Flowers was tugging on my flight suit for attention, but I pretended not to notice.

"First group!" yelled the Brit. Flowers and I and three other Marines from the platoon stepped forward. A corporal walked to my left side and snapped himself to my harness for a tandem lift.

"Who's flying with my sergeant?" I yelled above thumping helicopter blades.

"No one, Ma'am . . . we can't let an officer like you fly solo." And before I could protest, we were being dragged along the open field, boots toe-dragging the dirt until we were whisked into airy nothingness.

"Put your left arm around my waist, Ma'am!" the Marine said. He and I were in the first position; there was no one on the cable above us. I wrapped my arm around his waist and looked down to find Flowers in the third position, her head within a toe stretch of the Marine whose head I could almost touch with my own. Flowers was spinning in circles, and her screams had become ear splitting.

"Put your right arm straight out, Ma'am," the corporal said, "and we won't spin!" We were climbing to five hundred feet, and below me, Flowers was a whirl of green. Her black hair, which moments earlier had been neatly pinned, had come free and was covering her face as she spun.

I heard the Marine barking below my feet, "Sergeant, put your arms out."

"What?" yelled Flowers.

"Put! Your! Arms! Out!"

She finally relaxed her arms from their chest-crossed position and nervously extended them outward. She was now flying like the rest of us, face forward into the wind, and I knew this moment would change her forever, as the desert operation at Twentynine Palms had changed me.

★

As an officer, you're taught that when your staff performs well it falls upon you to credit the names of those within your staff responsible for the job well done, and this I did to commanders during staff meetings who praised our base newspaper coverage of their units. I would say, "Thank you, Colonel, I, too, was pleased with Sergeant Tripp's ability to get at the heart of the story." Or, "I will pass along your comments to Sergeant Flowers, who worked extra hard on that story." I remember when I was a sergeant how much it meant the day Major General Day's aide called our office at Camp Pendleton with a request that I report to the general's office; the general had personally thanked me for a feature story about the four-man fire team, the Corps' most basic combat infantry element.

To the New River CO, I did no differently in praising the talents of my staff. In fact, I passed along so many positive comments about Sergeant Flowers and the Sergeants Tripp that the CO was wondering why I was needed at all. Nothing the colonel did or said, from our first meeting when he let me know he did not like women in the Marines or warrant officers, fit the leadership guidelines taught at Quantico. His methods certainly didn't fit with the examples of leadership I had been exposed to throughout my career. I found myself reeling with confusion.

And just as you're taught as an officer to disburse credit, you're taught to assume upon yourself anything negative with regard to the actions of your staff. And so when the CO stumbled across a misspelled word or two in the base newspaper, it was, of course, my fault. When Sergeant Tripp's slide show of the air station, the one the colonel wanted shown to the Cherry Point CO one afternoon, became a disastrous event—upside-down and backward slides—the colonel had called me incapable of "making things happen." And, of course, he was right.

In hindsight, I had heaped upon my sergeants the enormous level of trust my Public Affairs officers had heaped upon me, and in doing so, I had assumed my sergeants, given any opportunity to shine before the CO, would act and perform to the same conscientious level I had as a sergeant. But sometimes, as they say, *shit* just happens. Tripp had previewed his slide show in our office several hours before he and I headed to the CO's office. I was just as shocked as he when somehow the slides were out of sequence and backward, and we suspected sabotage by one of his peers, maybe even his soon-to-be ex-wife. These were learning times for Sergeant Tripp, who was thirty-three, and for me, a new officer at twenty-eight, but the colonel, facing a possibility of a star in his future, didn't have the time or patience to grade on a curve.

Four days after the SPIE rigging adventure with Sergeant Flowers, I was promoted again, this time to *chief* warrant officer. I had returned to Public Affairs after the promotion ceremony and had dropped my purse on my desk. I was glancing over Flowers's slide choices for the new front cover of the base newspaper, when one of the sergeants poked a head into the office and said I was needed back at headquarters. I grabbed my purse and a notebook and headed back to the CO's office.

On the drive back to headquarters, I tried to imagine what new problem lay ahead. Had one of our New River Marines been arrested off base? Had there been a security leak of top secret material? Were we due for a high profile visit? A press conference? My office itself was in good shape, much better than when I had taken over two years earlier. We had updated the design of the base newspaper, *The Rotovue*, and the changes were garnering recognition by Public Affairs offices around the country. The staff was current with physical fitness tests, fitness reports, and other administrative matters.

"You're fired," the XO, the colonel's assistant, said. He was sitting behind a large desk, a desk too big for the room. To the left of his desk was the door that led into the colonel's enormous office, twice the size of that first apartment on Okinawa.

I was sitting in the chair the XO had pointed to when I reported at attention outside his door. Looking back, I wonder what expression my face conveyed to him. I hadn't known a Marine could be fired. The XO's face held an unmoved, stony expression.

"May I ask why, Sir?"

"No." He neither blinked nor unfolded his tightly gripped fingers, which were resting in a knotted ball on the top of his desk. "Return to your office ASAP and pack your personal belongings. Go home until you're further notified."

I could feel my body in the early stages of shaking. I could see the faces of Marines from my past life as a sergeant—those I had tried to emulate, and now somehow had failed. I felt paralyzed in the chair of the XO's office, as if I might never rise and walk again.

"And," said the XO as I pushed against the armrests of the chair for support in standing, "when you get back to your office, you're not allowed to speak one word of this to your staff. You're not allowed to tell them what has just happened to you. You will not enter into any discussion with them."

I nodded and felt myself unsteadily walking for the door. Outside, the shock of February cold was a relief. On the walk across the parking lot I whipped off my wool sweater. I needed desperately to feel something, anything.

I parked my car in front of Public Affairs and realized I couldn't even remember the drive back from HQ. Obviously, I had made it, but I had no memory of passing the theater or the post office or the flight line, or whether I had even made the mandatory stop at the flight line for taxiing aircraft. I trudged up the stairwell to the second floor, where my office was located. I heard voices from the pressroom. Flowers poked her head around the corner. I asked her for a box. She disappeared and returned with one too small for all my writing awards, personal notebooks, files, and the photos of Tom and Morgan I kept on my desk.

"I'll have to make a second trip," I said aloud to no one. I glanced up and saw Flowers standing in the doorway with a puzzled look.

"Ma'am? What's going on?"

"Can't talk right now, Sergeant Flowers."

"Can I help you with something?"

"You can help me carry these to the car." I handed her an armload of notebooks.

"Where are you going?"

"Can't talk about it right now, Sergeant Flowers."

"Well, you have to tell us *something*."

I brushed past her and headed for the stairwell. At the car, I loaded the box into the trunk and took the rest of my personal items from Flowers's arms. I closed the trunk. I hadn't wanted to look at Flowers, but I found this impossible. When I did, I saw she was crying.

"Look, Sergeant Flowers," I said, "I have orders not to discuss it . . ."

"I'll find out what's going on and I'll call you!"

"No! Marie, don't involve yourself in this. Just do your job and I'm sure you'll be all right. *I'll* be all right." Then I slid behind the wheel.

She tapped on the window. Reluctantly, I rolled it down. "While you were at headquarters," she said, "admin called to say you needed to stop in immediately for your new ID card . . . you know, because of the promotion this morning."

On the floor in admin, someone had taped an X with masking tape, and this was where I stood as a Marine disappeared behind a camera to capture grim history—what could be mistaken for a mug shot.

★

Two weeks later, I'm in this interrogation room at Military Police Headquarters, and the captain has finally turned off the tape recorder. The pages of her legal pad are draped over the top, and she's flipping each sheet backward, scanning, and all of this delay feels intentional. A stalling tactic.

She sets the pad on the table. Sets her pen on top of the pad and leans back into her chair. She has the relaxed look of someone resigned to defeat.

"Since you refuse to answer the question about you and General Hopkins," she says, "I suppose you're dismissed for now, although you should know that I plan to interrogate every Marine on your staff." I picture Flowers, the Tripps, and the others, one by one, marching into this tiny interrogation room. I can nearly feel the weight of them in this ripped chair, see the same tape recorder inched across the metal desk closer and closer to each, see them shrinking back into corners from which I have tried to pluck them.

The interrogation for now is over, but at first I'm not sure I can stand. And when I try, the fabric tear on my seat cushion tugs at my pantyhose so that I have to reach a hand underneath to free myself. When I stand to attention, I feel nylon spread open and the sensation of air as the hosiery run travels from the back of my upper leg all the way past my knee and into my shoe. The captain doesn't know any of this, of course; she is staring out the window.

After a moment of silence that is punctuated by a sigh, she

realizes I am still waiting for the formal dismissal. She turns from the window. "You're dismissed, Tracy."

"Thank you, Ma'am." I do an about-face for the door.

"Why Washington?" Tom asks as I lay out Morgan's clothes for the next morning. He will have to dress her and see that she makes it to the bus stop on time, or drive her to school as he did that morning.

"I have to do something to fix all this." On the drive home from the interrogation, the next course of action occurred to me. Of course Tom wants to know my plan. Of course he is entitled to know, but I can't tell him. I am afraid he might talk me out of my decision. Besides, haven't I already called Washington? My request for a meeting with General Boomer, in charge of Public Affairs, granted? "I got us into this mess and I have to get us out." And of course, I mean John Hopkins as well.

As a Public Affairs officer, I know how a court-martial for General Hopkins and me will play in the public eye. If reporters are still calling, eager to break a story, I can only imagine how they will fall over themselves if they uncover what this story is about. It is a story with all the makings of tabloid salaciousness: Marine general, a decorated war hero, faces his mistress, a junior, married officer, in a court-martial. Court-martial. The words conjure images of a firing squad, of one's rank ripped from the sleeves, of one's back painted with a broad yellow stripe, and of one being forced out the gates of military protection into wilderness.

At 5:00 a.m. the next morning, I prepare to leave for DC. I am dressed in a turtleneck sweater and jeans for the five-hour drive. My dress uniform hangs on a hook in the back seat. On the floorboard, a small makeup case, new pantyhose, and my black pumps.

In the kitchen, I dump ice into a glass and pour a Diet Coke.

I wait for the foam to settle, and then empty the can. Tom dutifully refills the ice tray. Neither of us is speaking this morning, and I am grateful.

I set the soda on a table by the door and head to Morgan's room. She has kicked away the blanket and looks cold and exposed in just her nightgown. I cover her. On the floor lies the silky shred of what she fondly calls her scratch, and this I place near the hand I know will instinctively reach for it when she stirs. I kiss her chapped lips.

At the door, Tom hands me the glass of soda. He kisses and hugs me as if this time *he* is afraid I might not be coming home. "You said we could get through this," I remind him.

"We can," he says, but I am beginning to sense some doubt, as if he is now resigned to what I have known all along about the weaknesses within our marriage.

I am back on Highway 258, driving north as I did the day before when my thoughts were on fleeing to Canada. Only this time, I won't be turning around until I accomplish my mission. I drive past the same tobacco fields and past the abandoned gas station with its *We're Closed, Please Come Again* sign. Ahead of me is open highway, and I relish the envelopment of darkness that feels appropriate given the secrecy of my mission.

For weeks now, life has felt anything but normal. After getting Morgan to the bus stop for school, I wandered around the house, doing little more than light housekeeping. I was used to having structured, although chaotic, days at Public Affairs. Without the immediacy of project deadlines, I didn't know what to do with myself. I didn't care about watching TV, wasn't able to concentrate long enough to read anything, and wasn't able to eat or sleep much. Sergeant Flowers's mother called one day from Upstate New York and asked after me on Marie's behalf. She said Marie was expecting a daughter she planned to name Morgan.

And I spent time on the telephone with my mother, who, after hearing the details of the affair with the general, couldn't say enough about how helpless she felt and how sorry she was for the stress Tom and I were under, and wasn't there some way I could just leave it all for a while and come home to rest and think about where I should go from here?

But the one person I wanted most to reach during all this time was John Hopkins, and I wouldn't dare make the call. I would have to give my name to his aide. I trusted no one at this point.

As I drive toward DC, I reflect on the events that have brought me to the decision I am about to engage. A few nights earlier, a woman staff sergeant who works at the air station called to say the CO's driver, a lance corporal, had learned of my affair with John from John's driver. She said John's driver had told the CO's driver that the general was seeing a warrant officer at New River. Since I am the only woman warrant officer at the air station, the CO easily made the connection. This rumor, the staff sergeant said, was fueled to credibility when the CO learned from one of my own sergeants—Sergeant Tripp's wife—that General Hopkins had once called my office.

Sergeant Tripp's wife and I had been peers at Camp Pendleton before our reassignment to New River, where I was now her boss. For two years since my promotion to warrant officer, we'd walked the slippery slope of transition that occurs when you find yourself suddenly working for the person who weeks earlier had been your peer; or the reverse, when you find yourself suddenly in charge of a staff who, weeks earlier, had comprised your best friends.

Now, as I drive toward DC, I am imagining this young woman inside the interrogation room. What will she have offered under oath? And isn't it often what is left unsaid that is sometimes the most damning? And then there is the dilemma regarding Sergeant

Flowers. Why did I allow myself, an officer, just days before being fired, to cross the line with Flowers? She was a corporal when we met at journalism school in Indiana during the early 1980s, and I, a sergeant. Still, in the two years since her assignment to New River, I have not allowed myself to be drawn into fraternization . . . that is, not until the day after our SPIE rigging experience.

The day after, Flowers and I went on a three-mile run together after work. We were training for the upcoming PFT. Flowers was worried she couldn't pass the test; she always looked in shape, but she hadn't seriously run in a while. Halfway through the run, we both stopped. My chest felt heavy with the February chill and dampness. As we walked, we talked. Flowers was separating from her husband, a gunnery sergeant. She had met someone new, she said, and was pregnant, certain the baby was this new man's and not her husband's, and we talked about the dangers of adultery charges her husband could bring against her and her Air Force boyfriend. She asked for advice—how I'd determined that going back with my husband at the end of last summer had been the right decision. I told her I hadn't known for certain. But then, out there on a cold, deserted highway that circles the New River Air Station, I gave away too much of myself, and John Hopkins.

You can't imagine how many times I have asked myself why I told Sergeant Flowers everything about John. Years later, during moments of self-examination, I would recall a moment that had occurred between a striking Air Force officer and me nearly a year before the confession to Sergeant Flowers. The Air Force officer and I, both Public Affairs officers and attending classes at the University of Oklahoma, were walking around the campus after dinner when suddenly he confessed that while stationed in Germany a few years before, he had been recruited by the CIA for intelligence drop-offs and pickups. There he was, blurting out the details about top secret missions. He was describing the fear of carrying a certain briefcase that was to be stashed behind a toilet in a German lavatory, and describing the suspicious looks he read into foreign faces along foreign streets as he toted briefcase after briefcase of classified documents to their drop-off points. "They told us in Virginia at training," he said in a hushed tone that night, "that one day we'd find the one person we could tell everything to." He grabbed my elbow and we stopped walking. "You're my one person."

Sgt. Marie Flowers became my one person. Looking back, I see a little of the repressed sixth grader leaking out: the child who felt compelled to embellish stories to impress her cheerleading friends when she felt them separating themselves from the girl with the crazed father who got tossed out of the gym during Friday night basketball games. Only this time, the story didn't need embellishing to be impressive; it involved real people with real careers at risk. I was twenty-eight—younger than my daughter is today, a few years older than my college students, but that is hardly an excuse. Telling Flowers—witnessing what my mind, anyway, was interpreting as her expressions of admiration, even envy?—created the sort of high I hadn't experienced since giving up alcohol. The more forthcoming with details, the more admiration and envy I read, and so I became higher and higher with each detail, became hooked as deeply as I always imagined I would be if ever I allowed myself to try, just once, cocaine.

Socrates said, "The unexamined life is not worth living." And this became the mantra I carried forth from the regrettable events that transpired in the months that were to follow, and in the years since. Motive. Just as a prosecutor for a murder trial must establish a motive, I have questioned myself repeatedly about my motives. Why am I about to tell my girlfriend about such and such? My mother? My daughter? My husband? And if the answer I receive is that this telling only feeds my ego, I make every effort to stop myself. Do I always succeed? Hardly. God knows, I wish I could tell you otherwise. What is it I have yet to master about the ego-driven monster that requires an equally monstrous feeding from time to time, only to produce the same sort of crash I get whenever I allow myself to binge on cookie dough ice cream with heaps of peanut butter?

When I look back on the day with Flowers, I can also so clearly now see how years of insecurities with my weight and with my failure to please my CO inspired this need to boast to Sergeant Flowers about the attention I'd received months earlier from a general. And I think I even see a young woman, one of few women officers on the air station and immersed in a man's world, who was starved for female companionship. After all, Flowers had just shared she was pregnant with another man's baby. Hadn't this prompted me to deliver a secret just as salacious? Whatever the reason, as a *leader*, I failed miserably that day.

Sergeant Flowers had listened in earnest to every detail just as I had listened to the Air Force officer tell me about his top secret CIA missions and briefcase drops. If Flowers and I had been sitting in my office at Public Affairs, I'm sure she would have plucked every lash and half a brow before I finished. I described for her how on a hot, June afternoon the previous summer, I had come face to face with John Hopkins at a change of command ceremony, and that this, aside from a shared glance and smile at the commandant's reception years earlier, had been our first meeting since our days in the Mojave Desert.

I had seen John first, standing near the bleachers and towering over Gen. Al Gray. He had glanced away from Gray, and that was when he had seen me. The corners of his mouth lifted, and then, as if catching himself, he had made a half turn away from me and moved in closer to General Gray. I headed for the other side of the metal bleachers. I noticed there was plenty of room near the top, but I was wearing a skirt and high heels and so I elected to stand to the side of the bleachers rather than make the climb.

After the ceremony, John was beside me, shaking my hand. In the background, the band was blasting the air with military march music, and he leaned closer. "Good to see you, Tracy, it's been a long time." A single silver star adorned each of his collar lapels. He hadn't changed much in five years, except that his face held less intensity, less firmness, and I wondered if this weren't because the rest of his career might require less control.

"And then what happened?" Flowers asked. I couldn't appreciate the danger I was putting us in by sharing this story, how she could be forced to testify against John and me in a court-martial one day, anymore than I had known that day while standing dangerously close to John on the hot tarmac of the change of command ceremony that in six months he and I would be facing threats of a court-martial. No, I couldn't have known any of that then.

Instead, I went on describing for Marie—for I think I was seeing her now not as a Marine, but as a woman, and a woman with whom I had once been friends before becoming the officer and she, one of my sergeants—how I had stared up at John and how I had tried to imagine how he might have looked as a cadet at the Naval Academy, in cadet uniform and in the shoulder pads of a Navy lineman. Even then, as captain of the 1956 football team, the team responsible for a tie with Army, he'd been designated as a leader by his peers. Now, he was standing before me in cammies and boots, smiling, as if we were old friends. His aide, a young lieutenant standing nearby, shifted his bodyweight as if uncomfortable with the scene.

"Yes, Sir," I said, "it's been a long time. Five years since Twenty-nine Palms." He had not released my hand, nor was he shaking it.

"I hate to hear that you and your husband have separated."
How had he known this?

"Yes, Sir, we have." He slowly withdrew his hand from mine and rubbed his chin, and then he stuffed his hand into a pocket. The other hand he used for talking.

"Is there any chance the two of you would reconcile?"

I shook my head. "No, Sir, there isn't. We've just grown too far apart over the years."

He nodded. "That's too bad. It happens though." He was hesitating, as if searching, and then, "I'd like to ask you something." The aide, perhaps sensing a tone of the too personal, shuffled out of earshot.

"Yes, Sir?"

There had been an uncomfortable pause during which, if I'm honest, I can't pretend I hadn't guessed or hoped what would follow. I wanted him to ask quickly before he changed his mind. I wanted to hear confirmed what I had suspected while up on the desert mountain with him that day so many years ago.

"Would you like to have dinner with me sometime?" And there it was. Confirmation. I had read the signs correctly all those years ago. And, I suppose, John had read whatever signals I had transmitted to him. I had been twenty-two then in the desert, and married. But wasn't I still married? Despite my separation from Tom, the Marine Corps considered this behavior conduct unbecoming an officer.

The general was waiting for my response, and thoughts were flashing with strobe-light speed through my mind: an intimate relationship constituted adultery; a simple dinner together, fraternization. These charges would ruin his career, to say nothing of my own, but then, he was a general, he knew all this; and maybe, just maybe, I've come to think in the seventeen years since, when you're someone like John Hopkins with stars on your collar and a Silver Star for bravery on your chest, you don't care anymore; maybe you look at every day since that jungle firefight in Vietnam as either a curse or a bonus, a gift; and maybe, when you're a young woman who since the age of eleven has been in love with the idea of measuring up, and in love with the cinematic vision of a conflicted general, notwithstanding her passion for *this* general standing before her now who is waiting for her answer—he had been a colonel five years ago when he taught her that challenges were victories not yet won, and she had marched into his office two weeks later with an expert rifle badge pinned to her left breast pocket, and now she was swarmed by the memorable image of those bees on a canteen cup—maybe you lose your head; maybe you say to yourself, *I'll never have to see combat to feel more alive than I feel in this moment.*

And so I gave him what he wanted, what I think he had always wanted from me. "I'd like that very much, General Hopkins."

Was he scowling? "Look," he said, leaning close enough that I could feel his hot breath on my face. He pressed a palm against his chest. "What I need to know is whether you'll have dinner with *me*, not the general." There was something so moving behind those eyes, something so pleading, something so conflicted. If I said no, I knew I'd regret it. I knew all about regret. Regret is not saying good-bye to your father as he lay dying from third-degree burns from a car accident; of starting into his dark hospital room to say, *I'm here for you, I love you, I forgive you,* when your grandmother grabs your arm. "Don't go in there, Tracy," she says. "Remember him as he was."

And your fiancé, Tom, saying, "Yes, don't go in there . . . I don't want you to go in there."

And now General Hopkins has asked if you can see beyond the stars.

"Yes, Sir. I can do that."

He smiled. "This could be trouble." He straightened until I felt him too far away. I wanted to reach up, grab a chest full of that camouflage uniform jacket, and yank him back into my space. He glanced toward his aide, who seemed to sense a signal and who was stepping forward. To me, "I'll call you tonight. You're listed, right?"

"Yes, Sir." And before I finished my salute, he had signaled to his aide, who snapped to the general's side, and I watched the two men walk toward the sedan marked for the general by a single star on the license plate.

★

Ahead, the road sign indicates that the exit for Interstate 95 north is a mile off. I suddenly realize I have been shivering and switch on the heater. The blast of hot air on my feet works its way through sneakers and into my bones.

Once on Interstate 95, I drive through the heart of downtown Richmond, passing tall tobacco smokestacks on the left. At times I am thinking ahead about the upcoming meeting with General Boomer, and at other times, I am lost in the past, in the painful moment when I confessed to Tom about my affair with John Hopkins.

The confession was made the afternoon I was fired and sent home. I had been on the telephone with the major from Cherry Point, and the major had asked if I knew a general at Lejeune. The expression on my face gave me away; Tom suddenly appeared by my side. His hand on my shoulder had felt hot and heavy.

I ended the call with the major by asking if I could call him back. And then I had slowly replaced the phone into the cradle, delaying as long as I could the confession I had to make.

"What did he say?"

I told Tom everything. He jerked his hand from my shoulder and stormed across the bedroom. He slumped into the chair. "Hopkins? Why *Hopkins?*"

Why? I reeled from the ludicrousness. "In his defense . . ."

"You're defending him?"

"He asked up front if there were any chance you and I would reconcile and I told him no. You know how things were last summer."

Indeed. Any mention of our time apart since our reconciliation drew a curtain of depression across Tom's face. Now though, my husband was looking curiously around our bedroom. He was conjuring John Hopkins, that tower of a man and war hero, as he thought John might have looked leaning against the doorframe, or sitting in the same chair where Tom untied his bootlaces each night, or how the general would have looked in our bed—for Tom's eyes had fallen there now. And I knew Tom was hearing things as well: the telephone busy signals last summer that he had complained about while trying to reach me from the BOQ; all the last-minute requests of him to take Morgan. Or, maybe I was wrong. Maybe these were only my thoughts.

The parking lot of the rest area north of Richmond is empty except for a semi that has been left running, the driver nowhere in sight. A woman with a child, both bundled against the cold, are tossing coins into a vending machine. The child pulls the lever and the selection thuds to the bottom.

Inside the head, I slip off my shoes, socks, and trousers. I am shivering, which makes it more difficult to balance on one leg and wiggle the other into pantyhose. My feet are swollen from the drive, and the high heels pinch. I slide on the skirt. Half-dressed, I lean over the sink to see better against the weak overhead lighting. I dab makeup onto the dark circles under my eyes. I slip into the shirt, fasten the tie to my collar, and decide to leave the jacket on a hanger until I get to headquarters. I take a step back to imagine what General Boomer will likely see in about an hour. I'm nothing like the smiling confident woman he met last fall, I think. Then, Boomer was the new general in charge of Public Affairs. We had met at a Public Affairs seminar that had been held in a hotel meeting room off base, and when everyone darted out for lunch, Boomer had surprisingly called me aside to say he wanted to see my offices at New River. I had driven us there, given him the nickel tour, and had driven us back to the seminar. What I hadn't been able to imagine then was how pivotal that day would prove to be.

I step back to the sink and rummage through my makeup case for eye shadow and pink blush.

Headquarters Marine Corps is a fortress of a building in the heart of DC, less than three minutes from the Pentagon. Inside HQ, I walk along the polished corridor to Public Affairs. I am early. When I announce myself to Boomer's secretary, a friendly older woman in a conservative suit, she says he is ready to see me.

Boomer's office is cavernous and heavily furnished with a large desk and a sitting area that includes a sofa and several occasional chairs upholstered in traditional patterns. The lanky general stands and smiles as I enter. He motions to the sitting area, but before sitting, extends his hand.

I sit on the edge of the left side of the sofa and watch the general fold himself into one of the chairs.

"Thank you for agreeing to see me on such short notice, Sir."

He crosses his legs and places his hands, one lightly over the over, on his lap, reminding me of a sympathetic minister or funeral director.

"What's going on down there, Tracy?" He is being polite. Of course, he knows what is going on. But I describe being promoted two weeks earlier to chief warrant officer and then being called back soon afterward to be fired. He shakes his head. I tell him of his predecessor's comments about my CO, and how I was warned that my career would suffer under the colonel. I tell him General Miller promised to watch for anything negative on my fitness reports, but that Miller is now, of course, retired.

"What can I do to help?"

"Sir, I realize I still have two years left on my contract . . ." and I take a deep breath. This is it. "But I would like to resign." There, it is out. If I resign, no one can force me to testify against General Hopkins, no one can force me to reveal the details of our summer affair. "I would appreciate whatever you can do to push it through." I am already feeling closer toward regaining some control over my life.

Boomer appears stunned. "That's not what you want, Tracy. You're an excellent Marine, a fine officer. Let me help by sending you orders for duty here in Washington. I can get you out of all this. You're the kind of Marine we need here at headquarters."

It sounds almost too good to be true, and for a moment I seriously consider it. For a moment. "There's just one thing I need to know . . ." he says. He is shifting his weight in a chair that looks too comfortable. "I just need to know if you and John Hopkins ever slept together." Now it is my turn to be stunned.

I know there can be only two reasons Boomer is asking: to fuel his own curiosities, or to confirm suspicions for the court-martial of John Hopkins.

"Sir, I've devoted nearly ten years to being a Marine. Every day has been a struggle to prove I belonged, that I was good enough. I've sacrificed time with my daughter and my husband to prove myself."

"But I'm telling you I can make all that go away. I just want to know what happened between you and Hopkins." Maybe it is reality smacking me in the face, but inside I sting from what feels like emotional blackmail: tell me what I want to know and I'll protect you. I am feeling less of a Marine in this moment than ever and even more like the walking caricature of incongruity. I have the sudden realization that I am somehow a woman who is regarded by every man in her life—Hopkins, my CO, the Silver Fox, my recruiter, my husband, even my father—as either worthy of protection or of destruction, depending upon the man.

No, General Boomer, I think, I won't give you the last bullet to aim at John Hopkins and a court-martial. I won't be forced into testifying about the details of our affair, or about how we met in restaurants near Swansboro and Emerald Isle in our futile attempts to be discreet. Nor will I testify as to dates or times or locations—or, for that matter, how many times we made love, nor to the intimate details of our telephone conversations. I won't tell you how I led John by the hand to my bedroom one night after dinner, how the general walked so lightly behind me on the hardwood hallway that I turned to satisfy myself I wasn't leading a phantom. Nor will I describe for you how I had taken a scarf from my drawer and draped it over the bright lamp on my nightstand, nor how John's enormous hands had fumbled with the buttons of my blouse so that I had been compelled to relieve him from the awkwardness and take over the moment of undressing for both of us: my hands unbuckling his belt and sliding his trousers over narrow hips to what would have been a pile on the floor but for my helping him from each leg and then matching the creases and smoothing the trousers across the top of my dresser. Nor will I describe the look on John's face as he took in all of me, how he had slumped into the chair, that same chair from which my husband blouses his boots each morning, and said, "You look just as I've imagined all these years." No, whatever evidence you amass without my testimony will only be a few telephone statements that will reveal dates and durations of calls John made from places like Rhode Island, his office, and from his general's quarters at Lejeune. Nor will I ever testify to being in his quarters, though John's driver—who met me in the driveway to lead me through the kitchen and upstairs to the general's bedroom—will, if required under oath. As will Sgt. Marie Flowers, if called upon under oath. No, if my CO lobbed a grenade toward John Hopkins and me, I am willing to jump on it for all of us.

"Sir," I say instead, "do you remember your visit to Lejeune last fall?"

"Certainly."

"Do you remember how during lunch, you asked for a tour of my offices at New River, and I had driven us there?"

He nods and something about his expression tells me he is leapfrogging ahead of logic to beat me to the conclusion.

"What you're not aware of, Sir, is that before you and I returned to the seminar, less than forty minutes roundtrip, rumors had circulated between the Lejeune and New River Public Affairs offices that you and I had stopped off for a romantic rendezvous." And this is true. I can't help but enjoy the shockwave exploding across the general's face. His hands grip both arms of the chair. His legs uncross.

"What?"

"That's right, Sir. I had one hell of a time convincing my staff that nothing inappropriate happened between us that afternoon. The harder I tried to convince them, the less persuasive my argument became, and yet, nothing happened between us. Did it, Sir?"

"Of course not!"

"You see, Sir, I've been plagued with rumors like this for two years now at New River. There was the visit from Gen. P. X. Kelley when he and I rode in his staff car to the flight line . . . there's this mess with Hopkins, and then our . . ."

"So you're telling me you and Hopkins never had a relationship?"

"No, Sir, I'm not saying that at all. What I'm saying is that it does little good to confirm or deny it. Denying a relationship with you didn't work . . . there are still Marines at Lejeune who hold onto what they want to think happened between us that afternoon. The more I protest, the guiltier *we* appear." His brows knit into a long, crooked line. I continue. "You, not Hopkins, might be facing a court-martial if someone initiated an investigation into what he *believed* happened. There can be no positive outcome for me, or for John Hopkins, or for the Marine Corps—no positive news spin if this thing goes to a court-martial. Please allow me to resign with dignity. My family needs me, Sir. They deserve the *whole* me for a change."

Boomer is silent for a moment. Then he stands, and I do as well. He reaches out to take my hand, and with a handshake commits himself to pushing forward a speedy, *honorable* discharge.

When I pull into the driveway that night, the front door opens and Morgan, dressed in her nightgown, shouts *Mommy!* Tom appears in the doorway and smiles when I smile.

I gather everything from the back seat, the jeans and sweater, sneakers and socks, and trudge up the sidewalk. "It's over," I say. He takes the heap from my arms, disappears inside the house with it, and when he returns, I am sitting at the dinette with Morgan on my lap. Between Morgan's snippets of her day at school, I describe for Tom the outcome of my meeting with Boomer. Morgan holds her wrist up to my face. "Look at my new sticker, Mom." On the inside of her tiny wrist is a silver star.

The next day I receive a telephone call from an admin officer at New River who says all charges have been dropped and that paperwork for an honorable discharge is being processed. I am torn between elation and a sense of great loss. What am I if not a Marine? How, I wonder, does John feel today, knowing he has dodged another bullet in his career?

I would prefer to wait out the three weeks of the discharge paperwork process at home, but the CO intends to punish me through humiliation: he issues orders for me to work in his headquarters office, attending to the most menial of admin duties, and to report each day to a staff sergeant, who is thankfully most gracious, given the awkwardness the colonel has placed her in.

She and I work well together, and in my last three weeks as a Marine, we complete a number of mind-numbing tasks. On the last day, she motions me into her office. "I want you to know that what they did to you is unforgivable, Ma'am. It was nothing short of a witch hunt." She hugs me and then pulls away. Her eyes are welling up with tears. "If they can do this to someone like you, what's the hope for the rest of us?" She nods in the direction of the CO's office a few doors down the hallway from hers. "You know, I think he actually has regrets."

The CO is standing behind his desk, looking over paperwork when I stop just outside his doorway. We lock stares. Two years ago, I stood at attention in front of that desk while he told me of the two strikes I had against me. I entered his ballgame handicapped. Now, he is almost smiling, although not the kind of smug bully smile you might expect, but the sort of respectful smile you imagine between two enemies who have battled hard against one another and survived, even if scarred for life. Maybe it is the afternoon light behind him, but he seems grayer than I remember, and as I walk out the door of the headquarters building and to my car in the parking lot, I think of how he reminds me of a white tiger, fighting extinction.

On April 15, 1987, I drive from the headquarters parking lot, and this time I am all too aware I am passing for the last time the air station theater and the post office. I am imprinting into memory the vision of Marines in flight suits and headsets on the busy tarmac, of them dashing into and out of hangars, waving in the approaching Huey and Cobra helicopters. I drive by the Public Affairs office and notice by the usual cars in the parking lot that Flowers and Sergeant Tripp are working overtime again on the base newspaper.

On this day, the first George Bush is president and the Cold War is over. What I won't know until years later is that General Boomer will receive two more stars and that John Hopkins will receive his second. Nor is it possible for me to know yet that John and General Boomer will orchestrate together the successful Marine ground force in Desert Storm, nor that I will never have an opportunity to speak to John before he goes blind and dies from diabetes at sixty-five, eleven years after my resignation.

As I near the Military Police gatepost and slow the car, a lance corporal emerges, wearing cammies and boots. She glances down at the fender of the car and, noticing the blue officer's sticker, snaps to attention. "Have a nice evening, Ma'am." And then she renders my final salute. I ease off the brake and feel myself slide into the wilderness of an uncertain future.

Epilogue

I would be lying to you if I told you I hadn't second- and triple-guessed the decision to throw away my career to save John's, and to save the Marine Corps lots of embarrassing headlines, not to mention my family from public scandal. I took some comfort in my decision when relentless media broke a similar story in Los Angeles shortly after my resignation: two Marines, a male officer and his enlisted female lover, were brought to trial over fraternization. The national headlines were scathing about how the Corps interfered with love. At the same time, a Marine from our Soviet embassy was under investigation for espionage, and Oliver North was still giving testimony on the Iran-Contra affair. Still, I found myself through the years wondering if I hadn't thrown it all away for nothing. Had the entire court-martial threat been of no real concern to John or to his career? After all, hadn't he survived other media scandals, the Oceanside brawls that made *Newsweek* and *Time* headlines? He never, to my knowledge, attempted to contact me, though I had this unshakable feeling in Okinawa, where Tom and I went a few months after my resignation, that others who knew us both kept him updated. In my mind, I've played out a scene during Desert Storm in which General Boomer and John, over dinner in a desert tent one evening, are reminiscing about the day a young woman fell on her sword.

The larger question forming in my mind as year after year ticked further beyond the resignation was: if given the same circumstances, would I take the same action *today*? For the longest time, I refused to answer it, refused to reexamine motives and actions, refused to accept there could have been any other way. After all, you can't ask a dead Marine if jumping on a grenade to save the platoon was the right thing to do. But if you could, I'm guessing she would say yes.

Halfway through recording this story, I suddenly realized I hadn't told Morgan anything about my life as a Marine, which meant she knew nothing about the circumstances around why I had enlisted at eighteen, or anything about the circumstances surrounding my discharge. She had been eight when I left the Marines, nine when Tom and I finally divorced. I had always feared and suspected that Tom, out of anger over the divorce, would one day blurt out his version.

After my honorable discharge, Tom was assigned to Okinawa for three years. A year into the assignment, I asked again for a divorce, and for all the same reasons I had at the beginning of the summer of 1986: I never felt Tom understood or appreciated my need to drive toward something, the need to accomplish something rather than to merely exist as his wife. And I suspected if Tom were to tell Morgan his version, it wouldn't include a mention of how I had sacrificed my career to save him, our family, the Marine Corps, and General Hopkins from public embarrassment. Sadly, in Tom's version, my passion—for my work and for John—had ruined us all. And maybe his version *is* closer to truth than mine.

I had other reasons for not wanting Morgan to know about that painful time in our lives. I hadn't forgotten how my parents' weaknesses fueled my rebellious spirit. And so my intent had been to build as solid a foundation under the woman Morgan looked to as a role model as I could. I was layering cement over the truth, fearful that a discovery too early in her life could crack the foundation beneath us.

For years after the Marines, I struggled with identity issues and guilt over a failed military career, and later, several failed marriages, as well as businesses that succeeded wildly during some years, failed miserably during others. Cliché as it sounds, I wouldn't trade any of these experiences. I grew most during the hard times, coasted too easily during the softer years. Sometimes I envy my friends with rock-solid marriages that have survived twenty, thirty years or more; sometimes, dare I say it? I pity them. But each of us has to find our way; each of us has to overcome our own demons.

In the end, at forty, two years after Morgan left home for college, I finally recreated the life I wanted for myself. I went to college to pursue my passions for writing and teaching.

But, immediately after the discharge, I'd plunged into depression, gained lots and lots of weight, and eventually resorted to antidepressants that helped to temporarily numb the mind-cyclone of *What was I, if not a Marine? What was I if no longer someone with something to prove?* I purposely lost touch with the Marines I cared most about—Sergeant Flowers and Sergeant Tripp. Although in the years since, I learned that Flowers did, indeed, name her daughter Morgan, and achieved the rank of gunnery sergeant before she retired. The Sergeants Tripp divorced shortly after my resignation. Nathan Tripp was promoted to warrant officer a few years afterward and eventually retired. Just recently, however, Nathan made local headlines after police discovered he'd shot and killed his new wife before turning the weapon on himself. Police found Tripp, now a Gulf War veteran, in his battle-dress uniform, in a chair in the basement, surrounded by a cache of weapons and explosives, a single shot to his head. I was overcome with grief, even guilt for not knowing until after his death that his father had been a highly decorated Marine, himself. What kind of selfish young officer was I that I didn't know this about the Marine who had been the most loyal? What demons had poor Nathan Tripp been fighting to live up to his father's expectations?

However turbulent my thoughts regarding my own failures, Morgan, I discovered years later, has little memory of me in a military uniform. She remembers me best in pinstripe suits and pumps, as a cellular phone sales representative who in six months was promoted to sales manager and a year afterward to vice president, thanks to a certain amount of self-discipline and work ethic I'd acquired in the Marines. And she remembers me later as the hustling real estate agent and as the returning college student.

Even though she couldn't remember me as a Marine, Morgan often used the fact I had been a Marine as an excuse to friends. "You know I can't do that . . . my mom was a Marine. She'll kill me if I do something that stupid." And this had rescued her from the peer pressure of tattoos and tongue and ear piercing, and during the night when three of her friends during a sleepover at a neighbor's had slipped out a bedroom window, leaving Morgan behind.

Today, Morgan is thirty-one. After graduating from a small university in Greenwood, South Carolina—just two weeks after I graduated from a small liberal arts college in St. Petersburg, and on my way a month later to graduate school so that I could teach writing on the university level—she took off for Los Angeles to pursue her dream of becoming an actor. She packed what clothing and furniture would fit into her Ford Explorer and into a U-Haul, and with her black schnauzer, Hanz, by her side, drove across country, stopping first in Dallas to visit her father.

Most days, Morgan is in acting classes or selling real estate with her boyfriend. Most nights, she bartends to make ends meet. A couple of years ago, I flew in from Tampa to tell her the truth about why I left the Marines, and about completing this book.

She met me at the bottom of the escalator in the LAX baggage claim terminal.

It had been four months since my last visit to Los Angeles, six years since her move there, and still I was finding myself counting the time backward three hours every time I looked at a clock. If it were noon at home, I was imagining her at 9:00 a.m. West Coast time on the way to a morning audition or to the gym; at 4:00 p.m., I pictured her finishing lunch al fresco somewhere in Santa Monica; and at 10:00, when I was slipping into bed with a book, I pictured her as she must look to the rich and famous who dined at the restaurant: another Hollywood starlet on the verge of her big break. I was living in the East on West Coast time.

Now, at the bottom of the escalator in baggage claim, where my daughter was grinning and nearly jumping with excitement, East was meeting West again.

Morgan drove us from the airport, weaving into and out of traffic on the busy 405. Once inside our favorite Westwood hangout, BJ's, that night, we ordered pizza. I looked around at the crowded tables of young people who were laughing or cheering the Dodgers on during a game that was being broadcasted from ceiling-mounted television sets around the perimeter of the restaurant.

"So how's the book coming along?" Morgan asked, even before biting into a slice of our Thai chicken pizza. Seeing her across the table was like looking into a mirror at the old me, or rather the young me. I thought back to the military ID card in my footlocker.

"That's one of the reasons I'm here."

Morgan lifted that one eyebrow of hers, the one that had taken her two years to train after deciding during her sophomore year of college that it might enhance her screen image one day to be able to raise an eyebrow. Now she was raising it at me, and I couldn't help but laugh.

And so there in BJ's, over pizza and to the background cacophony of cheering baseball fans, I provided a condensed version of the events you have now read. When I finished, Morgan
was looking at me as if she were sitting across from a stranger. I
guessed she was making mental connections, tying up the loose
ends of her childhood.

"But remember," I said, already searching for a way to repair
spreading fissures in the foundation, "I was the same age you
are right now."

There was this long silence between us during which I was
afraid to blink, afraid that if I did blink everything Morgan and
I had shared would vaporize. Children have such ideals about
their parents. Our children can't imagine us twentysomething,
passionate, and driven. Our children, just as I believed of my
own parents, believe we bring them into this world with all the
wisdom we can't possibly earn in life until sometime in our forties
or fifties, and even then, only if we're lucky. How unfortunate our
biological nature isn't contrived to allow us to hold off childbear-
ing until our forties or so. What better parents we might make.

I finally glanced away and up at the baseball game. I took a deep
breath, and when I gained the courage to look back at Morgan,
she was staring, arms folded across her chest, studying me. On
her face—that lovely face so perfect a combination of Tom and
me—was an expression I couldn't quite read.

"Are you okay with me telling this story?" I asked.

She unfolded her delicate arms and leaned across the table.
The trained eyebrow lifted high on her forehead, and she pointed
a finger accusingly at me. "Mom, you have to tell this story."

And so I have.